AN INTRODUCTION TO

JAINISM

Thoroughly Revised Second U.S. Edition

D1477002

BY

BHARAT S. SHAH, M.D.

THE SETUBANDH PUBLICATIONS
New York, U.S.A.

First U.S. edition   1992
First Indian edition   2002
Second U. S. edition   2002

OTHER BOOKS BY THE AUTHOR
(See the end pages for ordering information)

SETUBANDH LANGUAGE SERIES

A Prgrammed Text To Learn Gujarati

English For The Grandma And Her Children
(In   Gujarati)

A Crash Course to Learn the Gujarati Script

A Crash Course To Learn The Devanagari Script
(Hindi, Marathi, Sanskrit Languages)

Sanskrit: An Appreciation Without Apprehension (In Future)

TO MY MOTHER

Who

Did Not Have To Learn Religion

She Instinctively Knew It

Who

Does Not Have To Teach Religion

Her Own Life Speaks It

PREFACE

Jainism is a very ancient religion from India. Its latest prophet Lord Mahavira, 'the great conqueror' (of the self) was a contemporary of Lord Buddha, and he lived 2500 years ago in the same State of Magadha (today's Bihar, near Calcutta) as did Lord Buddha. Jainism has a sizable and powerful following in India, but because of its non-missionary nature, it is not well known outside India, although its principles are quite well recognized.

Mahatma Gandhiji's non-violence was rooted in Jainism. Vegetarianism follows from Jainism's respect for life in general. Jainism is known for its own 'Theory of Relativity' as applied to the philosophy and the truth. Its idea of 'Multiplicity of Viewpoints', advocates tolerance for other viewpoints, even though they may appear to be untrue. Jainism provides practical answers and explanations to many of our environmental and ecological dilemmas.

Such a vast religion cannot be covered adequately in a small work like this, which is neither a text book, nor a guide, nor an encyclopedia, nor an instruction manual. It is not an attempt to convert anyone. This book is primarily directed towards the Jain children born and brought up outside India, away from significant exposure to their mother tongue, to Sanskrit or to Jainism.

Many of these 'children' have completed their high school and college studies as well. They are in a unique situation. Their parents grew up with the so called eastern culture, religions, and the Indian language(s), including at least some Sanskrit. Even without any formal learning, these parents could manage well, thanks to their passing acquaintance with these.

Many of the first generation immigrants to the USA are from this group. They did not realize how little they themselves knew of their religion, until the time came to teach it to their own children. The parents who picked up their religion, maybe with some reluctance and resistance at times, now find themselves unable to teach it to their willing and eager children, in spite of great effort. They face an unprecedented situation.

They try to teach, to their youngsters who cannot speak or understand their mother tongue, something which is in Sanskrit and in other ancient languages which are strange even to the parents themselves, and to teach that in English, of which the parents have a limited mastery, if any. The situation in India is not encouraging either.

The traditional teaching methods and teachers from India can do very little to help these students. The classical way of learning by memorizing without understanding is not very appealing. Learning by participating in the festivals and the rituals directed towards the adults, is at best boring, and at worst a torture for this second generation.

Busy schedules of parents and of children, together with an interest in the 'success', and an intense effort necessary to learn a foreign language (English) and culture, required to facilitate assimilation, leave very little free time. Long driving distances and a low priority assigned to the religious and linguistic pursuits, compound the problem.

Not that there are no good books on Jainism in English. There are many, written either in India or elsewhere. The former are for the Indian intellectuals already familiar with their content, and the latter are meant for the western readers familiar with the Judeo-Christian thought. Our second generation belongs to neither of these groups. It is not familiar with either philosophy.

It is for them that this book is written. Its purpose is to give them some understanding of the basic principles of Jainism, its relevance in the modern world, and to explain to them the rationale behind the rituals and festivals that they attend either voluntarily or under somewhat less ideal circumstances.

I do not claim to be a scholar of Jainism. As a matter of fact, I know very little of it, and I practice still less. But I am deeply impressed with whatever little I have learned. My parents and teachers were kind enough to explain what is what, and that's what I would like to share with our younger men and women. I am a parent, father of two college age 'children', and as a parent, I think, this business of instilling religion into our future generations is 'too important to be left to the scholars alone'.

As I had expressed my thoughts in the preface to 'A Programmed Text To Learn Gujarati' parts 1-3, I would say this again. I do not think that all Jain children have to know everything about Jainism. That's their decision. But, should a Jain youngster, or anyone else, want to learn about Jainism, it should be available to him or to her. It is their right, and is our duty, to make it available in the form accessible to them.

It is every child's birthright to know
his/her own language, culture, and religion.

For my part, I would be immensely pleased if one of the readers of this book will be sufficiently interested and capable to study and then to translate into English poetry, some of the most beautiful and lyrical Jain writings filled with deep philosophy.

The book is tailored to its readers. The most interesting principles are covered in the first part. Then based on these principles, explanations of some religious practices are given in the second part. Unlike what is traditional, the lives of the prophets and the apostles, a description of Jain canonical literature, and a small sample from it are kept for the third and the last part, which is almost entirely filled with many interesting and enlightening stories.

The style has been kept simple and conversational. Emphasis is on under-standing and thinking, rather than justifying everything. Long Sanskrit words have been broken down whenever possible. A Glossary of terms has been appended. The treasure Chest towards the end is a collection of gems, and the parents will do well to go over that with the students, emphasizing its charm, rather than some technicality.

In general, differences among various sects have been ignored. The difference between Jainism and other Indian religions has been underplayed, and Jainism has been presented in a broader perspective, in the context with other religions of the world. Parents and teachers may want to stress some aspects of Jainism not emphasized here.

I would urge the parents and the teachers to encourage their children and students to learn their mother tongue. It is futile to convey one's culture and religion in a totally strange language, no matter how good the latter may be. In my experience, learning the mother tongue makes learning the culture and religion easier and interesting.

ACKNOWLEDGEMENTS

I would like to thank Dr. Andrew Baeder, and Ms. Binny Mehta from Parsippany, NJ. for a meticulous copy editing. Dr. Premchand Gada, Mr. Manubhai Doshi from Chicago, and my friends Drs. Lila and Mahendra Shah for a very thorough review. Manubhai volunteered on his own, gave a thorough critique, and provided important factual corrections and suggestions. Dr. Gada did the same together with Manubhai on several prolonged long-distance phone calls from Lubbock, TX.

I also appreciate the comments from Mr. Kiranbhai, Prof. Madhusudan Kapadia, and Ms. Sarita Gandhi from Boston, MA. Understandably, not all suggestions can be carried out, even though they are gratefully acknowledged. The responsibility for the content of this book is entirely its author's, and no endorsement or approval from the reviewers is implied.

My nephew Akshat, a newly arrived ninth grader from India, enthusiastically assumed the responsibility for word-processing and proof reading the book. My brother Hasmukh, his wife Kashmira, my sister Aruna, all participated in typesetting to varying extent. My college-going son Nikhil extensively reviewed and proofread the book, and made it readable for the second generation. My daughter Manisha gave general help, and my mother provided me with her constant blessing, and encouragement. While the book was being prepared, as always, my wife Usha had to put up with being ignored, and had to pick up the slack for me in social and many other obligations.

I can never forget the selfless dedication shown by my friends, and the strangers who became friends, in helping me out in distributing the book – A Programmed Text To Learn Gujarati – and to make it reach into various parts of this globe. Most did not even accept my token of appreciation. They spent their own money on telephones and for postage. They turned a potential disaster into a glorious success, and thereby gave me courage and strength to embark upon this venture, and to look forward to many more.

Bharat S. Shah, MD.
Great Neck, New York.

v

PREFACE TO THE FIRST INDIAN EDITION

In the ten years since its first publication, *An Introduction to Jainism* has been extremely well received by students and teachers from all over America and England. What is most rewarding and encouraging is the warmth with which the students themselves have embraced it. Using the book as a resource, they have prepared and staged countless games, quiz shows, and competitions at various Jain conventions and other events.

The greatest testament to the book's success comes from the fact that it has reached its popularity among students simply by word of mouth. They have recommended, suggested, and sent this work as a gift to their siblings, cousins, and fellow students. I am sure that it will also be received equally enthusiastically in India.

Many have commented on the simple but impressive cover page, especially its bold color scheme. Not many could recall that the red and white stripes are the colors of the ceremonial Jain flag, displayed all over our temples and in the *Upashrayas*. Recently a new formal flag representing various sects has been adopted. However, I have purposely avoided emphasizing the differences among various sects, which are ultimately united in the same fundamental principles.

There is an interesting story behind how *An Introduction to Jainism* came to be written. On the first day of *Paryushana* many years ago, I was fasting without taking any food or water. I remember I was in my office at the hospital trying to concentrate on my research work, albeit with some difficulty. Having been brought up in the Godiji Building, next to the flagship Godiji Jain temple in Bombay, I was fortunate enough to have been immersed in an environment where Jain thoughts saturated the air.

That compelled me to ponder the meaning and purpose behind fasting and other rituals. The Jain word for fasting - *Upavas* - literally means "stay close to" the word of the Jinas, that is! Not eating is a minor point of the *Upavas*. I was not supported to be working! My pride in being able to continue working despite my fasting melted away in the warm memories of the great teachers and preachers I had come across. With due modesty, despite my background, if *I* had forgotten that, then how many of us in America would remember it? And who would explain it to the dozens of children doing *Aththais* (eight) fasts in every town? So, I thought to myself, "Why don't I do that?

Although not a scholar of Jainism, I figured that I knew enough for a parent to teach children. I had studied in Babu Panalal Puranchand Jain High School. It used to remain closed during the eight days of *Paryushana*, so that we could listen to various religious discourses and lectures. Every year in *Samvatsari Pratikraman*, I had heard repeatedly that **it is an *Atichara* (a transgression), not to do something that needs to be done, even though one is capable of doing it.** I couldn't bear to commit that *Atichar* myself. And so, an outline filling every inch of an entire page was prepared on that very afternoon. A Shravak was reborn, and *An Introduction to Jainism* came into being.

January 2002.

PREFACE TO THE SECOND U. S. EDITION

This edition of *An Introduction to Jainism* has been thoroughly revised to correct mainly typographical misprints, leaving its contents largely unchanged. Relatively inexpensive first edition is still available, and is usable. This version is published in a sleek, easy to handle format. It is produced by employing an innovative technology currently revolutionising the publishing world, called Print On Demand (POD), wherein the book exists only on a computer, and is produced, literally one copy at a time as required, thereby obviating the expense and hassel of maintaining an inventory in face of un unpredictable demand. Terrorist attack on New York's Twin Towers a year ago once again attests to the need of tolerence and non-violence taught by Jainism.

Bharat S. Shah, M.D.
Great Neck, New York
September 2002

TABLE OF CONTENTS

PART I : FUNDAMENTAL PRINCIPLES.

PART II : PRACTICE, RITUALS AND RATIONALE

PART III : PROPHETS, PUPILS AND PEARLS

PART III : PROPHETS, PUPILS AND PEARLS

(CONTD)

ORDERING INFORMATION

☆ ☆ ☆ ☆ ☆ ☆ ☆ ☆ ☆ ☆ ☆ ☆ ☆ ☆

JAINISM   I

FUNDAMENTAL   PRINCIPLES

1. RELIGION. THE ART OF LIVING

It is auspicious and fitting, that I am beginning to write this Introduction to Jainism on Mahatma Gandhi's birthday. He was born on October 2, 1869. His whole life was based on non-violence, which is one of the most important teachings of Jainism.

The fact that you have started to read this book indicates your interest in Jainism, in religion in general, and possibly, in the Indian culture and tradition. It is likely that you are born in a Jain family, or at least one of your parents is Jain, or you are just curious. Even if you are not a Jain don't be concerned. In as much as all religions attempt to achieve the same purpose, you will learn something about whatever your family religion may be, if any at all.

The reason I say 'if any' is that not everybody believes in religion or in God. It is up to an individual to decide for oneself, and as such there is nothing good or bad about it. Being born into Jainism or other religion does not necessarily make you a better person, any more than buying a good world map would make you a better traveler.

Religion is for practicing. It is not just for knowing, or for memorizing. By "practicing", I do not mean blindly following the rituals of fasting, going to temples, chanting, or doing this, or not doing that. It is not for arguing about, fighting for, or killing over it either. Even though a lot of blood has been shed in its name, religion is a very worthwhile thing.

Religion is not meant only for the old, the weak, or the deprived, poor and ignorant people. It does not have as much to do with what happens after death as it has to do with what goes on before that. Simply stated, religion is the art of life and of living.

If we all yield to our selfish desires, we will want more and more, and soon we will be killing one another. Since we are all basically similar, it is easy to understand that if I do not rob you of your possessions, you will probably not rob me, and we can all live peacefully and happily.

Or rather, if I **give** you what I have, so much the better. If we think more about this, as prophets have done, we can see clearly that:

Being good to others is the best way to be happy.

So far so good. Any book on any religion can be closed and put away once this basic truth is understood. The trouble is, we accept this only superficially. In practice, we either forget it or ignore it. Believing in this basic truth requires faith, be it in Nature, in God, in Justice, or in one's own self. Religion shows us a way to further develop that faith, and to facilitate its application to the everyday life.

Even without ever having read a single book on religion, based on common sense alone, we can understand the reasons why we fail to see our good in someone else's. Number one is, we do not think. If we do think, we think of the immediate gain rather than of the long range effects. We may be blinded by our desires, passions, and so on. Therefore, even if we can see and understand, we may not act accordingly.

It is human nature to be selfish, and hence self-destructive. Not being good to others cannot make us happy. Therefore, control over our selfish nature is the only way to happiness. Jainism puts a great deal of emphasis on this. Other religions also seem to make this point.

But different religions have to do this in different ways. For, over the centuries human nature has not changed, but circumstances have. This has forced religions and prophets to make the same point in different ways, all of them being right in one way or the other, and at one time or the other. They all deserve to be respected. Jainism goes to a great length on this point.

What is this Jainism, which advises self-control, non-violence, and tolerance towards other points of view? And yet, why does it fly banners with the Swastika on them? Why does it make you fast?

2. WHAT IS JAINISM?

You are familiar with the ending '-ism', as in Hinduism, Communism, Capitalism, etc. meaning 'a school of thinking, believing or doing something'. Other examples are, Impressionism, Modernism, and so on. Jainism is the Jain way of thinking, believing, and practicing.

Those who practice Jainism are called Jains. They are civilian men, women, and the monks and the nuns. The word 'Jain' does not rhyme with 'pain'. Ask someone to show you the correct pronunciation. You can try saying 'pain' pronouncing 'pa..' as in 'particular', then you will be close.

Actually, 'Jain' means 'follower of Jina'. The Sanskrit root word 'Ji' means 'to conquer'. Therefore:

*The Jinas are the conquerors, and
the Jains are their followers.*

Jinas did not conquer anybody else. They conquered themselves. Before you say, 'Big deal! Even I can do that!', let me explain. It is indeed very difficult to conquer other lands. Many conquerors have walked on this earth before. They have done a lot of destruction, and have caused many deaths. Many of these conquerors had subsequently fallen victims to wine, (bad) women and other vices. Even after controlling the whole world, they failed to conquer themselves.

Controlling one's own self is extremely difficult. But you are right, when you say, that you can do that too. Jainism agrees with you. It says:

*Anyone can conquer oneself and
become a Jina.*

Before we leave the other conquerors, let us give them due credit. No one can just pick up a gun or other weapon and go wage a war. Modern soldiers go through very rigorous basic training before being sent to the battle front. We need discipline and self control to fight the enemies outside us. For the enemies within us, total mastery over the self is absolutely essential.

Interesting as all this may be, you might wonder, "How does the Jinas' conquering themselves concern us? What do **we** get from them?" Having conquered themselves, i.e. their enemies within, the Jinas were able to stay on the path of the common good, of religion, and of truth. Moreover, thanks to their endless kindness and love for humanity, they showed us that path - the path to salvation, liberation, Nirvana, or what the Jains call our **Moksha** (from Sanskrit Much, with 'u' as in Bush, meaning 'to free').

Not only did they show us the way to cross the great ocean of our woes, they even built us a dock, or 'Tirtha'. This **Tirtha** is the Jain religion consisting of monks, nuns, and the civilian men and women followers. Because they founded the Tirtha, these Jinas are also known as **Tirthankaras** (Sanskrit, Kru = to do), or in other words, 'the founders of the religion'.

The Tirtha is also called **'Sangha'** or the union, of the four components mentioned above. Don't worry. Jinas or Tirthankaras do not derive one more name from the word Sangha. However, you may know that there is a last name 'Sanghavi'. A Sanghavi is one who takes the Sangha to the Jain holy city Palitana, where the holy mountain Shatrunjaya (Shatru = an enemy, Jaya = to conquer) is situated. The Sangha bestows that title of great honor upon that person.

So, if you see the last name Sanghavi or its derived form 'Singhavi' you know that that family is Jain. Also, you may see 'Jain' as a last name, and one more called 'Shravak'. These four always indicate a Jain family, and together, they account for 1-2 % of all Jains.

If you are a Jain man, you are a Shravak. A Jain woman is called a Shravika. These are very important words, not only from a linguistic viewpoint, but also from a religious viewpoint. These words actually tell us what a Jain is and what he or she does. The word 'Shravak' comes from Sanskrit.

3. A SMALL HISTORICAL TIDBIT

There are several reasons why I tell you all the Sanskrit derivatives. First of all, so that you can understand things better. Secondly, you can see that Sanskrit is quite interesting and important to learn. And lastly, you can appreciate that it is not at all difficult.

Your mother tongue, if it is Gujarati, Marathi, Hindi, Punjabi or Bengali, is a daughter of Sanskrit. You may like to know, that English is a distant sister of Sanskrit. Both of them belong to the same family, called 'Indo-European Languages', or languages of India and Europe.

If you learn Sanskrit, you will be able to appreciate your mother tongue better, and you will learn something more about English and Latin. Almost all Hindu scriptures and a few Jain ones are in Sanskrit. Jain literature is mostly in Ardha-Magadhi, while the Buddhist literature is in Pali. Both of these are daughters of Sanskrit, and are mothers of Gujarati and other North Indian languages. Magadha, from which 'Ardha-Magadhi' derives its name, was a State in Eastern India, near Calcutta. It is known as Bihar today.

Magadha is the birth-place of both, Buddhism and Jainism. Actually, about 2500 years ago (500 years before Jesus Christ) Lord Buddha, and the 'founder' of Jainism as it is today - Lord Mahavira (again, Maha = great, Vira = a warrior), lived there during the same time period.

Buddhism as a force vanished from India, taking roots in the neighboring Sri Lanka, China, Japan, Thailand, etc. A Buddhist monastery (where monks live) is called a Vihar, and at one time, there were so many of them there, that the whole State came to be known as 'Vihar', or modern day 'Bihar'.

This digression was important, and if you patiently continued to read, you are a good Shravak, or 'listener'. It comes from the Sanskrit word 'Shru' meaning 'to listen'. One who listens to (or reads) the word of Jinas, thinks about it, and puts it into practice, is a Shravak. Now you know what Jainism means. You also know about the Jinas, the Tirthankaras, and about the Tirtha or the Sangha.

4. UNIQUENESS OF JAINISM

I would urge you not to start flipping the pages of this book, to get to what you may call the 'main point'. If you do rush through, and even succeed in finding that point, you may still misunderstand it. This journey is as rewarding as its destination. Since we are going to practice what we learn, we should learn properly, with a stable mind, without any restlessness.

There is no single holy book of Jainism, which you can quickly read like a cookbook, and start acting according to what it orders. You may be interested to know that the Bible is not one book either, but is a collection of several books. The word 'Bible' itself means 'Books', as in 'bibliography', etc.

Hinduism has many books finally distilled into the Bhagavad Gita. Buddhism has several books, Judaism also has several books. Islam does have only one holy book, the Quran. It is not absolutely necessary to have one single religious book. It is true, a single book may simplify the life of a follower, but not necessarily so. Soon, with the changing times, the book may become difficult to live with.

The Indian tradition, especially Jainism shows a lot of respect for the individual, and puts a great deal of responsibility there as well. Jainism does not talk in terms of 'Thou shall not...do this or that'.

In Jainism there are
no orders to obey!

No religion promising to liberate you, can begin to do so by asking you to be a slave. This or any other writing in this book is not meant to criticize any religion, but is meant only to point out some differences, without implying any comment about what is the right or the best way.

Jain scriptures emphasize two phrases, which are very important to understand. One is 'Yatha Shakti' meaning 'according to strength' or 'within your capacity' (Yatha = as, and Shakti = strength).

The other phrase is 'Vartamana Joga' or 'Prevailing Conditions' (Vartamana = existing, prevailing; and Joga= Union, or a set of circumstances). In 'Joga', the 'o' is pronounced as in Bold. 'Joga' comes from

Sanskrit word 'Yoga' meaning a union, of mind, speech, and body. In a spiritual sense, Yoga means a harmony of thought and action. Contrary to what appears to be, the physical exercises are only a small part of Yoga.

Taking these two phrases, Yatha Shakti and Vartamana Joga together, it follows that one is supposed to practice Jainism with due regard to the existing conditions, and to one's own capacity. Someone can say, that in America or somewhere else, it is beyond our capacity to practice any part of Jainism at all! In a way, (s)he is still following a doctrine of Jainism. No one is forcing you to do anything. You practice it, only because you know and believe that it is good for you.

For our ills, the Jinas have given us a medicine. We cannot simply throw it away, just because we don't like its taste or color. Jinas have done their part. We are not required to please them, but we have to try to make at least ourselves happy. We can begin to do that, if and when we are ready. The Jinas can only guide us.

Mercifully, they do tell us what is worth doing, what is worth practicing and developing, and what is worth avoiding. But they do recognize that we are not all alike either in physical strength, knowledge, understanding and commitment, or circumstances.

Even among the four parts of the Sangha, the level of practice for the civilians cannot be the same as that for the monks. Shravaks and Shravikas strive to practice the best they can, hoping to reach the level of the monks and the nuns (Don't worry, you don't have to. But why not?) and then aspire to become the Jinas themselves, if they so choose to.

You can see that there are innumerable levels of practicing Jainism. This makes the religion very democratic, and it can accommodate all kinds of people, treating them as equals but being mindful of their limitations. One should always try to move up to a higher level.

As a religion which respects the individual, and which recognizes the potential of each and every person to become a Jina, Jainism does not believe in the Caste System. Indian tradition describes four castes in a descending social order. Brahmins are the scholars and teachers, then Kshatriyas are the warriors, Vaishyas are the business people, and Shudras are servants.

Jainism does not believe in the Caste System.

A Jain may be from any of these castes, yet still be called a Shravak or a Shravika. Lord Mahavira's first eleven disciples were Brahmins. Many Kshatriya kings, and even poor Shudras were accepted by Jainism. Today, most Jains are business people. But once again, they are all Shravaks or Shravikas.

We can understand that Shravaks and Shravikas can become monks, and then aspire to become Jinas. Just as in a democracy, everybody can vote and someday hope to become a mayor, senator, or the President. These officers of the government do command our respect, even though everybody is equal. Similarly, there is a hierarchy of sorts in Jainism, to guide us in our steps towards the Jinas.

More about that later. First, let us look at how we see ourselves, and then try to find the way towards becoming a Jina.

5. OUR HAPPY SELVES

Regardless of whether one believes in God, either as the creator or otherwise, our interest in Him is rather selfish, that is, 'What does He do for us?' Since Jainism puts so much emphasis on the individual, let us now look at ourselves.

The easiest way is to look in a mirror. There we see ourselves exactly as we are, with all our clothes, jewelry and what not. We may think that we have plenty of these, or we may want more. We can work more, and earn more in order to buy more. In doing so, we may have to outsmart our friends and colleagues.

We can build muscles and be strong enough to beat up anyone. We can acquire power, become a mayor, or a governor, and so on. We can buy more and more land, and on that, build bigger and bigger houses, and live happily ever after, right? Well, if this were so, all the kings, presidents, and rich people would have been the happiest people amongst us.

Lord Mahavira was a prince, as was Lord Buddha, and they had untold wealth and everything else that one could possibly want. Yet, deep down they did not feel happy. The same thing happens to us also. If we do not have wealth, we want it, and once we have wealth, we want more. Ultimately, this only makes us unhappy in the long run.

But there is one big difference between what we do and what Lord Mahavira and Lord Buddha did. When we are not happy with what we have, we try to get more, and yet some more, hoping to be happy, some day. When Lord Mahavira saw that wealth and pleasures did not make him happy, he decided to give up all that he had, and set out to find true happiness. When he did find it, he told us how we too can make ourselves really happy.

We may think we are happy, but we really aren't. We don't even realize that we are all essentially unhappy. We don't even know what true happiness is. Yes, if one has nothing to eat, nothing to wear, or has no place to live in, one can be unhappy. But we do not have that problem, nor did the prophets have that. What we get from a good house, good clothes, good food, and good movies is pleasure. Happiness is not quite the same thing as pleasure.

When we help a fallen person get up, or when we give a hungry man something to eat, or when we save someone from difficulty, we feel good. This is real happiness, even though in gaining it we may have had to give up some of the wealth and pleasures that we could have acquired. But we don't mind that. We are the masters of all we have. Or are we? We have to earn our wealth, protect it, fight for it, and at times, lie awake with the fear that something may happen to it.

Even we ourselves, handsome, beautiful and strong as we may be, are not safe. We all get ill, grow old, and some day die. The more we pamper our bodies with pleasures, the sooner all this may happen. So, how can we be happy? We can find happiness by finding our true selves.

OUR TRUE SELVES

Physically and chemically, a dead body is not much different from what it was just before death, only the life is gone. This life, this energy, is called Atma (= Self, the soul). When we say 'we', we often refer to our country, or town, or house, and in the narrowest sense, our bodies. As a consequence of this, when we talk about self-improvement, we mean nothing more than improving our income, or getting a new bathroom, or joining a physical fitness program.

It is easy to appreciate that we ourselves are separate from our country, car, or house. A little more thinking will make it clear that 'we' cannot mean 'our bodies'. Our bodies are not living things. The Atma is the living element. Consciousness is not a characteristic of non-living things. We are conscious, sensitive, intelligent beings, capable of thinking, analyzing, and improving ourselves. 'We' should refer to our 'Atmas', and not our 'bodies'. The Atma is like the battery for our machine. Jain and other Indian religious traditions make this distinction between the body and the Atma very strongly.

Atma is the divine element, without which only a dead body remains. The Jinas tell us that the liberated souls had the same Atma as we have, just as water in a glass is the same as there is in an ocean. Their liberated Atmas, and the Atmas that are within us are one and the same. There is nothing extraordinary or spectacular about their Atmas that puts them above everyone else. Fundamentally, all Atmas are the same in all beings.

Thus, each one of us has a Jina hidden inside us, waiting to come out. That is the divine light within us. The Atma in our body can shine with divine light, only if we don't confine it and smear it. A mirror in our room can reflect the sun and can shine just as much, only if we keep it clean, free from dirt, and leave the door and windows open.

The door and the windows around our Atma can be opened, and the dirt from our mirror can be cleaned. Jinas have taught us how the dirt gets there, and how we can remove it. They saw the dirt, and they realized that a diamond buried under dirt and coal does not even look like a diamond. It has to be cleaned, ground, and polished. Then it will shine freely. We can all aspire to this.

6. STEPS TO OUR ASPIRATIONS

All Shravaks and Shravikas are potentially equally capable of becoming monks, nuns and Jinas. The Jinas or Tirthankaras are the Supreme beings. They are the liberated souls. Their mission is accomplished. They are free from all the worries and woes of the world, and of the existence. They are called the Siddhas, literally meaning 'accomplished'. The Monks and the nuns are Sadhus, or those who are trying to achieve their liberation. The Sanskrit word Sadh means to try to achieve, to strive, to persevere, etc. Thus, Monks are 'Sadhus,' and the nuns are called 'Sadhvis.'

Sadhus, Sadhvis, Shravaks and Shravikas together constitute the Jain Sangha, or Tirtha, established by the Tirthankaras. Among the Sadhus (and Sadhvis), there are teachers and preachers. One level higher among Sadhus is the Upadhyaya who is like the Director of Education. He is the one who teaches the other Sadhus.

The highest post in the Sangha is that of the Acharya who is the only one authorized to preach to the Sangha. Others may preach in his absence. There may be several Upadhyayas and Acharyas at one time. Jainism does not have an equivalent of a Pope as a spiritual head of Jainism.

But we are not Sadhus! Why should we worry about all this? Well, there is a good reason for that. If Shravaks are supposed to be good listeners, then whom do they listen to? Jinas? They are not even here. The Jinas' word comes to us via the Acharyas, Upadhyayas, and Sadhus. They are our guides, our Gurus. They not only read the scriptures, they think about them, write about them, practice them, and preach them. Their teachers are Jinas themselves. Jinas gave the knowledge to their disciples, and in turn the disciples gave it to their disciples, all they way down to today's Acharyas.

You may be tempted to say, 'Why don't we just read the scriptures ourselves?' You can, and you should. But when you are sick, it is easier to go to a doctor, than to read medical textbooks and journals. You can, if you want, become a doctor and read those too. In our spiritual search, we go to our Gurus, and try to follow in their footsteps. They arc thc stepping stones. To be like them is what we should be craving for. They are the most aspired beings called 'Parameshthis' (Parama = most, highest, Ishtha = appropriate, good, desired).

THE KINDS OF KNOWLEDGE

The word from the Jinas or Tirthankaras does not come from them after they are liberated ('dead'). Now you can easily understand why we write 'dead' in quotation marks. It is the body that dies. The Atma, being an energy, is immortal. Even then, an Atma has to have a body, in order to verbally communicate with other as yet body-bound Atmas. The Jinas proclaim and spread their message while they are still physically alive, but after they have reached the highest state of knowledge, called 'Kevala Gnyana' or sheer or pure knowledge.

Kevala Gnyana is the highest of the five kinds of knowledge (Gnyana). What we get by reading, or listening, or going to school is Shruta Gnyana (Shru = to listen, you do remember that, don't you?). Inherent common sense is called Mati Gnyana (Mati = sense). Then there is a knowledge of what's happening everywhere (Avadhi Gnyana). The fourth is the knowledge of what is in the other person's mind (Manaha - Paryava - Gnyana). And then, the Kevala Gnyana. You don't have to memorize these.

Those who have achieved the Kevala Gnyana, while they are living, are called Arihantas (Ari = enemy, Hant = one who has slain. Compare the word 'hunt' in English. 'Hant' is also pronounced as 'Hunt', with a dental 't'). All Arihantas are also Jinas. They become Tirthankaras only if they re-start the religion, as Lord Mahavira did. When they die, they all are called Siddhas.

I understand this is somewhat difficult for you, but it won't be much longer now. The effort we are putting into this, is nothing compared to what Jinas have suffered in finding a way to help us. In a way, we are going over all this, in order to understand and appreciate what has been done for us and to be thankful to them for that. Let us first pay our respects to the Sadhus (Sadhvis), Upadhyayas and Acharyas, who are ahead of us on our path to becoming Siddhas.

13

7. A PRAYER TO THE FIVE ASPIRED BEINGS

Namo Arihantanam	I bow to the Arihantas
Namo Siddhanam	I bow to the Siddhas.
Namo Ayarianam	I bow to the Acharyas.
Namo Uvazzayanam	I bow to the Upadhyayas.
Namo lo-e Savva Sahunam	I bow to all the Sadhus in this world.
Eso pancha namukkaro	Bowing to these five
Savva pavappanasano	Is Destroyer of all sins,
Mangalanam cha savvesim	And among all holy things,
Padhamam hava-i mangalam.	The first and foremost it is.

This is the most fundamental and most widely known Jain prayer, called the **Navakara Mantra**. It is also used as a chant, especially to calm oneself down when one is overcome with fear, anger, stress, or grief. Many Jain functions, meetings and rituals begin and/or end with it, or may incorporate it. One can either count 108 threaded beads saying this Mantra 12 times, one line per bead (12 x 9 lines = 108), or 108 times, one whole prayer per bead.

There is a reason for having exactly 108 beads. That number corresponds to the total number of all attributes or qualities of the five aspired beings. Therefore, it figures prominently in many Jain rituals as well.

Note that there are nine lines in this prayer called Navakara (Nava = nine), and in it we pay respect to the Pancha (five) Parameshthis (most aspired), that we ourselves can aspire to be. Sharvaks and Shravikas are not included, because it is they who aspire to be any and all of the five.

Although becoming the Siddha is the highest aspiration, we bow to the Arihanta first. The reason is, it is the Arihanta who teaches us. Siddhas do not. Also, becoming an Arihanta is difficult, to put it very mildly. Once you become an Arihanta, it is only a matter of time before you become a Siddha.

Now you know about Jainism in general, about its characteristics including equality, its hierarchy, its most aspired and worth emulating teachers, and its students. You may be wondering why we still haven't started talking about God. Isn't He supposed to be the main point of any religion? Arihantas are not God, because Arihantas are supposed to be human beings, nor are the three kinds of monks considered to be God. Are Siddhas God?

To answer that, I have to tell you how Jainism views the universe, and God. That is Jinas' word also. Once you understand that, you will understand what the Jinas tell, Acharyas preach, monks, Shravaks and Shravikas practice, and why. Meanwhile, continue to be a good Shravak. If you continue to read and listen, everything else will automatically follow.

8. GOD

One cannot separate God from religion. All religions talk about heaven, hell, and God. It is God whom they try to please, or at least try not to displease. The reason being that He is the almighty, merciful and yet ferocious and ruthless authority. He created the world, and can easily destroy it, if and when He chooses to. He is always watching everything we do and don't do, even in the darkest corner of the world and in our minds and in our hearts.

He is the one to whom, some day, we will have to give our accounts, when He will sit in judgement for us. He will then either put us in the heavens, full of all pleasures, or will throw us into hell, full of unbearable and endless misery. One is supposed to stay on the right path shown by religion, so as to end up in heaven and nowhere else. What you do and how you behave in this life are very important considerations.

This God is the God of Moses, of Abraham, of Isaac, and is the Father of Jesus Christ. He is the Fire God (Ahur Mazda, after whom the car Mazda is named) of Zoroastrians (Parsis), and is Jove or Jupiter of Homer. He is Allah of Muslims. You cannot bear to look at Him. He is too bright and blinding. He is burning hot. He is frightening to behold.

God in Indian Hindu tradition decides to split Himself into at least three aspects. Brahma - the god of creation, Vishnu - the god of day to day management, and a protector of the world, and Shiva or Shankara - the god of destruction before the next creation. They are all friendly and almost human, even though they are very powerful and are aspects of God.

Vishnu and Shiva have wives or consorts, Brahma is a bachelor, but being the creator himself, he created a daughter Saraswati, the goddess of learning. Although very pretty and lovely, she is an eternally pure virgin. Even though a virgin, she is our mother. We cannot be her master. In the Indian tradition, we cannot be a Master of Science, or of the Liberal Arts, etc. It is inappropriate to be the master of one's own mother.

Then there are the gods of rain, fire, wind, water, and so on and so forth. The religions that believe in The God are called **monotheistic** (Mono = one, Theos = God). On the other hand, Hinduism with its multitudes of gods is called **Polytheistic** (Poly = many), but *wrongly* so. Wrongly, because there are many gods, but only one God. There are many people and religions that do not believe in God (they are called **Atheistic**, A = none), some people do not believe in any organized religion, and they are called **'non-believers'**.

Where does Jainism belong in all of this? It is a no-nonsense, matter-of-fact, strict and straightforward but democratic and individualistic religion. It does believe in the world order, and talks at great length about the non-living and living world. But it does not dwell on the beginning or the projected end of the world and of the universe.

Jainism does not believe that someday, someone sat down and created everything. The question comes up, where was (S)He standing or sitting while creating? Who created Him or Her? Jainism calmly says that this world had no beginning, and has no foreseeable end. Mind you, it does not say that the universe will not end, or that it did not begin. We don't know, so 'no comment'. Some people have misinterpreted this, and again erroneously, called Jainism Atheistic, or non-believer in God.

I will try to explain more. It is fascinating to talk about God. Over the years, innumerable people have tried to talk about God, without ever really succeeding. God defies all descriptions! When you talk about God, everything you say may be true and untrue at the same time. To start with, God can be He or She. God can be present everywhere and yet no one is able to see Him. He creates everybody, but He is created by us!

I admit that the above is the silliest piece of writing you ever came across. At the same time, many will call it brilliant also (all this is not mine). We are not talking about me, we are talking about Him. What do I mean by 'He is created by us'? Let me explain.

No other religion 'knows' anything more about the Creation, any more than what Jainism does, which is nothing much to begin with. When we do not know something, either we keep quiet, or we make up stories. Not only religions, but even science does that. That's why theories are being overthrown all the time. Don't get me wrong. We are not calling anyone, especially other religions, a liar.

Nobody was present at the time of creation, so no one can tell us what happened. Since the creation till now, birth, death, planets, seasons, day, night, and everything else seems to operate in a very organized manner. This seems to be good for us. We do not know who or what operates all this, but it cannot just happen by itself. Whatever that good power or force is, we call it God.

So who runs the universe? God does. Who created it? God did. And who created God? We did! Do you understand? Don't worry if you don't. No one really understands. We are all thoroughly confused, so much so, that many of us don't even realize that we are confused.

The simple point is, God is an idea, like love, or happiness, or liberty, or gravitation. Therefore, there is not much difference in whether you believe in God as the creator, or you don't.

God is a wonderful idea.
Jainism is not against It.

We may not understand how or why it rains, but we do not have to have a rain god to make it rain. It just rains! In the same way, we may be rewarded for our actions or deeds, both good and bad; yet, we do not need to have someone sitting up there to distribute justice and to dole out our reward or punishment.

When we punch a wall, it hurts our hands. Every action causes its own reaction. Our deeds determine our fate. Whether this is done directly, as in a reflex (when you step barefoot on a burning cigarette, you immediately withdraw your leg), or through the agency of God, it is not really relevant for us. Now do you see why the wise and the merciful Jinas avoided getting into all this?

Jainism would not quarrel with you if you believe in God as the creator of the world, or as the administrator of justice. All it says is, you don't have to have someone like that. The Jain religion is very tolerant. One of its main points is just that, tolerance.

That principle is called 'multiplicity of viewpoints'. Different people looking at the same thing will see it differently (as in the story of seven blind men and the elephant. Ask someone, if you don't know this story). Even though they may describe the thing differently and in an apparently contradictory way, they may all be right.

When someone disagrees with us, and we *know* that we are absolutely right, we should remember that (s)he can be right also, even if we cannot see how. Moreover, both of us can be wrong too.

Once we appreciate this, our intolerance would disappear. There is no need to fight with someone who we think is 'dead wrong', or 'stupid'.

We do not have to kill someone just because (s)he follows a different religion, or does not follow any religion, or believes in this, that, or in no God at all.

This tolerance is the basis of non-violence towards one another. In fighting for the truth, by killing someone who sees something differently, we will only destroy the truth. But if we listen to different viewpoints, and try to understand them, we will be that much closer to the Truth, which is the same as God, according to many, including Gandhiji.

Don't torment yourself over trying to connect the Truth with God. Just as all rivers eventually meet in an ocean, all such spiritual concepts eventually meet in God. Truth is also God, so is Beauty, and so is Love.

You do not have to finish this book before you can start practicing Jainism. Even if you do not understand it at first, please continue to go to temple, religious school, the rituals of Puja and Pratikramana, and to the celebrations of the festivals. But do ask questions, and continue to ask, till you find some satisfactory answers. You will be surprised to find out that not every body understands why they do certain things. Don't argue with them, just listen.

9. THE CYCLE OF LIFE
REINCARNATION

Realization that what we so fondly call 'ourselves' is not quite us, is only the beginning. That is only the beginning of a long and arduous journey to find our true self. That is the path from the Atma to the 'Paramatma', or from the soul to the 'great soul'. Along that path, we aspire to be Sadhus, Upadhyayas, Acharyas, Arihantas, and finally, Siddhas. On that path, we may make wrong turns, take wrong exits, and experience vehicle malfunctions. We may fall in love with a beautiful picnic spot, or may get in stuck in the mud.

After any break, we may wrongly go back to where we came from. Sometimes, we forget what we started out for in the first place. Every time, we wake up, ask our guide (Guru), and start all over again. One lifetime is not long enough for this journey. Not even several hundred lifetimes. These cycles of birth and death cease only when we become a Siddha.

Our fate depends upon our deeds. It is well known that what we do to others, comes back to us. We have heard the proverb 'You reap what you sow'. But in the Indian and Jain traditions, we mean more than that, much more. Let me explain.

Very few of the religious doctrines can be called scientific in an accepted sense, but I will give you a scientific example to make a point. We know, or accept that life is an energy. When it leaves us, only a dead collection of matter, called 'body' remains.

The body feels no pain, physical or emotional. It can be buried, or burnt without a second thought. That's the end of it. What about the Atma, or the life? Does that also die at the same time? When a light-bulb blows, the electricity does not die with it. The electricity remains behind, and it can light up many more bulbs and can run other appliances.

The tradition believes, that in the same manner, the Atma leaves a body, and takes up a new life in another body, whether it be human or otherwise. This is the so-called **Principle of Rebirth.** Now the scientific example I promised.

It is accepted that, matter can neither be created nor destroyed. It can only be transformed into another form. The same is also true for energy. It can neither be created nor destroyed. It can only be transformed. We can burn fuel to produce heat, which can boil water to produce steam, which can run a turbine generator to produce electricity, which in turn can produce heat to operate an iron, or a toaster, or an oven. Thus, the cycle continues.

If life is an energy, the same rules can apply to it also. Life can never be created or destroyed, but it can only be 're-cycled'. The principle of re-birth cannot be scientifically proved or disproved at present, but it does make sense. It should be considered only a concept, just as God is a concept, and Atma is a concept. Some religions accept God as fact, while Jainism simply accepts Atma as fact, rather than as a concept. The contradiction here is only apparent. Faith does not separate a concept from a fact.

According to the theory of Rebirth, the Atma leaves the body when one dies, and is reborn in another body. This body could belong to another new human being, or animal. The Atma may also be reborn in hell, or in heaven as a god or a goddess. Although it is possible to be born as plant life also, the plants are not able to think or practice religion anyway. Even from the four others mentioned above (viz. Human beings, the gods in the heaven, the creatures in the hell, and lastly, the animals) in a practical sense, only the humans are capable of that. This is our best chance.

You may have seen the Swastika symbol. Its four prongs represent these four groups of life – gods, humans, animals, and the creatures in hell. The Atma can go easily from one into the other. We will talk more about Swastika elsewhere.

Depending upon the deeds of all its 'host' bodies, the Atma goes into one life form, and into another, and into still another. In each birth, it is either happy or unhappy, as directed by its (there is no 'he' or 'she' for Atma) deeds. This cycle of birth and death repeats itself over and over again, until the Atma gets rid of all its deeds and is liberated, that is, it becomes a Siddha.

10. THE NINE ELEMENTS

Jainism talks at great length about the soulless body, other non-living things, the living things that are the Atmas, how the Atma gets trapped in a bondage and how it is set free. This discussion covers the **Nine Elements**, or the fundamental points.

When Atma is in a body, it can do good and bad deeds. Under appropriate conditions, these stick to the Atma, or fall off. For example, a greasy mirror will attract dirt, while a clean mirror won't. On the other hand, soap may remove grease and dirt, making the mirror shine freely and brightly again.

The Nine Elements are :

(1)   Living (Atma)
(2)   Non-living (body and inert matter)

(3)   Bad deeds
(4)   Good deeds

(5)   Conditions favoring bondage (the 'Grease')
(6)   Conditions favoring freedom (the 'Soap')

(7)   Bondage
(8)   Breaking of bondage

(9)   Liberation.

We already talked about the Non-Living and the Living. The latter is the Atma, and since its fate depends on our deeds, let us talk more about the deeds, or Karmas.

22

11. THE REIGN OF KARMAS

Jainism has devoted serious thought to the union of the non-living body with the living Atma. The inherently free Atma is said to be 'bound' to the body because of its actions or deeds, called Karmas (from Sanskrit, Kru = to do). Once all the Karmas are gone, the Atma is free again. The concept of Karma is very important.

The living and the non-living are the first two of the Nine Elements. The good and bad Karmas constitute the third and the fourth. The remaining five Elements concern the bondage and liberation of the Atma from the body, specifically, the factors affecting both these processes.

Karmas include whatever we do, speak, or even think. They are either good or bad. The bad ones are called sins or **Papas,** and the good ones are called **Punyas.** There is no English equivalent word for 'Punya', which is exactly the opposite of sin.

As you know, it is a Papa to hurt or kill someone or something, to lie, to cheat, or to do anything that would make us do bad things, e.g., taking alcohol or other intoxicating drugs. In addition, there are bad aspects of our personality, viz. anger, greed, desires, undue attachment, and so on. These are Papas too.

A greedy person accumulates more and more wealth etc., regardless of what (s)he has to do to get it. An angry person is 'mad' and has no judgement, and is not capable of distinguishing good from bad. A person with too many desires soon falls slave to those desires. These desires can never be satisfied by fulfilling them, any more than a fire can be extinguished by pouring gasoline over it.

HOME OF THE PAPAS

We are tempted to do anything for our loved ones and for our country, because we are attached to them, or we have **Raga** (liking) for them. On the other hand, we hurt someone because of **Dvesha** (dislike) for that person.

When you develop Raga for someone or something, you develop a desire for that person or thing. If that desire is satisfied, you want still more; if it is not, you get angry. If you do get what you want, you wish never to part with it, you are attached to it.

> *Jainism considers Desire (Kama), anger (Krodha), attachment (Maya) and greed (Lobha) as the four greatest enemies within us.*

The Hindu tradition uses the word 'Maya' to mean 'an illusion', and you may see it commonly used in that sense in your school books and in general interest magazines. Jainism uses that word to imply 'attachment'. The difference is not as great as it may seem at first.

Because both these traditions consider the Atma as the real thing, any attachment to physical objects of desires is naturally considered to be an illusion. Although any attachment to these objects is as troublesome as a mirage in the long run, Jainism recognizes the objects themselves as real, and simply warns one against getting attached to them.

When we add Raga and Dvesha to the four great Papas mentioned above, we have six enemies. There are five more that we will talk about later. They come from not doing the five of the greatest duties of a Shravak. That makes eleven enemies. Add to that quarreling (**Kalaha**) and still six more, for a total of eighteen 'abodes of sin', or **Papa-Sthanaka** (Sthana = a place). Papas are better avoided to begin with, otherwise you really suffer.

Jainism discusses in great detail, eight kinds of (bad) Karmas. In general, they block or cloud our knowledge and perception, or may cause us grief or pain, and may not let us succeed in our ventures.

Be especially careful not to accumulate Papas. Once you acquire them, there is no way out but to suffer, suffer like hell, literally. Even Tirthankaras and other Siddhas had to suffer to burn out their Papas, before being liberated.

THE PUNYAS

As opposed to the Papas, there are Punyas. Whenever you help someone, give to charity, follow religious practices, or control your selfishness, etc. you accrue Punyas.

Why should we care whether we accrue the Papas or the Punyas? Well, because we are responsible and accountable for all our actions, whether good or bad. No deed goes unrewarded. Bad deeds are 'rewarded' with punishment.

Punyas can earn you a good life. You can get wealth, good body, and lot of pleasures. But these are not long lasting. Good times end very quickly, or at least it feels that way. So, while the good times last, don't waste them. When your fortunes are good, help others. It is very easy to commit Papas, when you have everything, including a lot of free time, an idle mind and selfish friends. Punyas are soon replaced by Papas.

Thus Papas are bad, and Punyas can turn into Papas. Therefore our aim is to do away with both of them. It should be remembered that Punyas do not make up for the Papas. They do not cancel each other out. Let's say you run a charity, but you also cheat on your taxes. You may be elected to be president of that charity, but you could also go to jail for tax fraud. Avoid Papas at all times.

Punyas are useful in avoiding Papas. Actions that generate Punyas are good for practicing the right behavior, and to keep us out of trouble. The Punyas are accrued during reading the scriptures, and that can teach us the right conduct. We can learn to be careful.

What about the Papas that we commit without knowing or realizing, or without really meaning to do any harm? Do they also stick as badly? Not quite. We will talk about this and other related issues as we go further.

For now let us conclude this chapter by saying that Karmas are the root cause of our woes, and are the cause of our ignorance and our wandering through the cycles of birth and death, or Sansara. They are the obstacles between us and our Nirvana or Moksha.

13. BINDING ATMA TO BODIES–
THE GREASE

The Karmas are done by the body, and it would seem that they should not affect the Atma, which is only an observer, or an innocent bystander. But, as we already saw, they do affect it. Karmas need a cementing substance, just as dirt attaches to a mirror with greater ease if the mirror is smeared with some grease.

If you are walking through a clearing in a forest, trying to go somewhere, the forest shouldn't stop you. Now, you may like some part of the forest, maybe a wayside lake full of lotuses, and you may decide to spend some time there. Or, you may be hurt by a thorn, pricking your foot, or some other part of your body. You get annoyed, irritated, and angry enough to decide to get rid of all the thorns. Either way, you remain where you are.

The forest sticks to you thanks to your love (= Raga) or your hate (= Dvesha). Raga and Dvesha are the cement, or the grease that make Karmas stick to the Atma, that is otherwise very clean, pure, and shining. Actually, when Raga and Dvesha (likes and dislikes) go away, many Karmas become unnecessary as well. Good deeds are generally done with detachment, or out of concern for someone else rather than for oneself. Therefore, they are less sticky.

If Karmas are carried out without the like or the dislike, with a neutral, detached attitude, they do not burden the Atma. The Hindu holy book Bhagavad Gita talks about detachment in a very interesting way. Although a few orthodox Jains may not like my saying this, I would urge you to read that marvelous book.

WASHING AWAY THE PAPAS : THE SOAP

The best way to avoid future suffering is to stay away from Papas. Our usual excuses when we do something wrong are, 'Mom, I didn't know', or 'I didn't mean to', or 'Gosh! Is that what I did?', or "I'll never do it again", or, 'I am sorry'. The same excuses and answers apply in the case of Papas also.

Sometimes we do the wrong thing, without meaning to, or out of laziness, carelessness and apathy. Or we even try to do the right thing without learning to do it, or without practicing. At times, we do it the wrong way, or at wrong place or wrong time.

Often, we don't think. Impulsive acts are very dangerous. Sometimes we are not able to think. We may take alcohol and other intoxicating substances like drugs, to forget our worries. But this is actually the best way to multiply our problems. Instead of making us forget our worries and ourselves, religion helps us find our true self, which is potentially no less than that of Lord Mahavira. Why throw it away?

When we cross a road, we look both ways. We should always be on the lookout for danger. Before we meet someone, we glance in the mirror to see how we look. We should always look at ourselves, our actions, and our thoughts to see how we are doing. 'The price for liberty is constant vigilance', remember?

We should be alert to not harming others, especially when there is no reason whatsoever for hurting someone. This watchfulness is called **Jayana**. You don't have to hit every animal that passes by. You don't have to drive the car over that 'stupid squirrel'. You don't have to step on every roach that you see. Maybe, if you keep your room clean, free from cookie crumbs and candy wrappers, you won't get any roaches in the first place. Don't punish the poor roaches for your own fault!

Another way is to recite, as a checklist, the sins that we are most inclined to commit. We will look at it later. When one sin is found, we should try harder to avoid it the next time. It is always a good idea to apologize when we commit a sin. True repentance goes a long way. Jains apologize by saying **'Mich-chhami Dukkadam'** (May my bad deed go in vain). We will talk more about this later. It is of no value to apologize, unless you are determined not to repeat that same wrong act.

One more way to avoid the Papas is to do something good instead. It is generally hard to do good work in bad places, in bad company or when your mind is filled with bad thoughts. Read good books, go to good places, and keep good company. That will keep you or help you to stay on a good path. Find the right path and stick to it. Martin Luther King, Jr. said 'If a man has not found something that he will die for, he does not deserve to live'. Find a good cause. Even if you cannot help others, you can always help elevate yourself.

14. GOING THE RIGHT WAY
ACCRUING PUNYA

The least that happens when you are doing something good is that you are not doing anything bad at that time. Being charitable and helping others may be difficult at times, and it may require you to give up something. I am talking about being good only to yourself and in doing so, you will gain a lot.

We are told that the Atma is immortal, and we take that on faith. On the other hand, there is no doubt that we, as a body, are going to die sooner or later. Death is like Candid Camera. It will catch us some day, when we least expect it, and make fools out of us.

I do not mean to threaten you with death. It is indeed a friend and a blessing as well. It makes life precious. One who wastes his life has no reason to be afraid of death, because he is already dead. On the other hand, one who lives his life well, never really dies. All prophets say that. Believe them.

Unlike all plant and animal life, human beings are capable of listening, thinking and doing something. A healthy body, with a healthy mind, together with good fortune is a rare combination indeed. Very few people get it. Hardly a handful of them will bother to listen to the word of Jinas or of any other prophets. If you are a real Shravak, half your battle is already won. My heartfelt compliments to you!

Jainism describes in detail, many Punyas and the ways to accrue them. There are rituals (to be discussed later), to stabilize the mind, to enumerate and revert from the Papas, to visit the temple to see the idols of the Tirthankaras and to do their Puja (to worship them).

Also, there are the eight holy days of **Paryushana** during which we draw our energy scattered everywhere and concentrate it into ourselves. We accomplish this by religious studies, fasting, giving to charities, and by atoning (apologizing) for our misdeeds. We will go over this later on.

For now, let us talk about what a Shravak should do. Since you know quite a bit about Jainism, and its teaching about the Atma, the Karmas and its view of life, you will have no trouble understanding what follows.

28

FIVE GREAT VRATAS OF A SHRAVAK :

There are five main vows, called 'Vratas', that a Shravak is supposed to do. When we talked about the 18 Papa-sthanakas, we left out five. These first five Papa-sthanakas come about by transgressing or violating the five Vratas (principles or vows) I am about to discuss. So let us look at them very carefully. Each one can be and has been a subject of countless books by Jain and other writers; but we will go over these only briefly. These are the most important principles of Jainism.

(i)   Non-violence

The first Vrata is Non-Violence, or **Ahinsa.** Since all living things are equal, and are interchangeable by rebirths, and since all are potentially capable of achieving the same Siddha status, a Shravak respects life in all forms and shapes.

For the monks, these vows are absolute, while for householders they apply in a gross and general manner. This is the reason why these vows are called 'gross' or 'minor' for Shravaks, even though they are major in their importance. For Sadhus, they are 'minute' or 'absolute'. We have to remember the phrases Yatha Shakti (within capacity) and Vartamana Joga (depending upon the circumstances) discussed earlier.

The householders have to make a living, and for that they have to buy and sell various things, and use animals to carry burdens. They have to cut and cook vegetables. They may have to lend tools and weapons to others for their use. In the Jain view, whether we do something, or we get it done, or we encourage someone else to do it, it is all one and the same thing. Karana (doing), Karavana (getting done), and Anumodana (cheering along) lead to the same outcome (Karma).

Do not misunderstand this. Killing anything yourself is certainly worse than having someone else do it for you. It is also worse than cheering someone else along. The point is, even cheering along someone in doing a violent deed is as bad as actually doing it.

In as much as all killing is first done in the mind, and in talk, Jainism forbids killing of any kind, even in thought or in words as well. It also advises against non-physical violence, e.g. insults, abuse, and emotional torture.

When we think more, we can see that many of our actions are hurtful to others. Our bad handwriting is one example. Poorly given directions is still another one. Not cleaning up after ourselves is also an example of subtle violence. Keeping someone waiting for us to arrive for an appointment is also a violent act. You can think of many such examples.

The non-violence of Gandhiji, Thoreau, Martin Luther King, Jr., and lately of the people of Eastern Europe and the Soviet Union in peacefully resisting or overthrowing their governments, is directly and indirectly rooted in Jainism.

Farming and fighting a battle to defend one's country are violent but essential endeavors. Also, practice of medicine and surgery fall under the same category. In as much as doing, getting done, and encouraging someone else to do it are same, common sense and non-rigid interpretations should be applied. Still, all violence should be avoided as far as possible.

One of the most serious acts of violence is intolerance towards those who do not agree with us. Such intolerance can lead to actual physical violence and wars as well. Jainism advocates tolerance based on the principle of the Multiplicity of Viewpoints. Our practice of Vegetarianism also naturally follows from non-violence. Let us talk about these two important aspects of the Vrata of non-violence now.

15. TRUTH AND MULTIPLE VIEWPOINTS

In the Broadway play 'Fiddler on the Roof', one character says something and the hero says 'You are right!' Another character says something quite the opposite of the first one, and the hero again says 'You are right'. A third character wonders out loud, 'How can both of them be right?' to which the hero responds, 'You are right too!'.

The above is of course a joke, but sometimes jokes bring out the truth better than anything else can. When two parties quarrel, they both must believe in something very strongly. There is some truth on either side, beacuse no side is absolutely wrong. The truth may consist of bits and pieces from both of these, and from many other sides. Without any of these, the truth as we see it, would be incomplete. Being tolerant of the viewpoints of others is more important than just being a vegetarian out of respect for other life forms.

Intolerance is violence.
It violates the other person's right
to be himself or herself.
And it violates the truth,
over which neither of us
have a monopoly.

Jainism respects this right of freedom of expression and belief, and it puts forward the doctrine of 'Multiplicity of Viewpoints' and of 'Relativeness of the Truth'. It goes under various names, viz., **'Anekant Vada', 'Syad Vada'** and the related **'Naya-principle'.** All these terms are not synonymous.

Together, these principles are so important that Jainism derives its other name **'Syad-Vada-Darshana'** from them. This principle provides one explanation for why Jainism is a non-missionary religion. It does not try to convert anyone to its doctrines, because that would be against those doctrines.

We are all lost in a forest trying to find the way to get out. If we waste our time in bickering over who is right, we'll never get out. On the other hand, left to our own, all of us will be able to get out, in one way or the other.

Truth is not always easy to find. Our eyes, ears, skin, and our mind can deceive us. Even when we agree on something, we all may have different ideas about what we agreed upon. That's why we see so many contract disputes in the courts.

What may appear to be the
same, may not be;
and what appears to be different,
may actually be the same.

When we say, all mothers are the same, we don't mean that our mother is the same as a female dog. At the same time, a bitch may care as much for her puppies as our own mother cares for us or at least, the puppies need their mother, just as much as we need ours.

Even opposites are not
always opposite of each other.

Republicans and Democrats may argue all their lives, and yet they are trying to do what they think is best for the country. To a New Yorker, Chicago is in the West, while for a Californian it is in the East. The gas pedal makes the car run, and the brake pedal makes it stop. But they both work together to take you to your destination safely. On a steering wheel, the left hand pushing it down and the right one pushing it up, are both turning it in the same, counter-clockwise manner.

Because nobody is perfect, everybody has a chance of being right. If we insist upon our truth, we will be dead wrong. The truth may not change, but our perception keeps on changing. By burning the bridges that can lead us to the truth, we only stifle ourselves.

It should be pointed out that when we decide to be non-violent, honest, tolerant, understanding, and environmentally conscious, it is not someone else that we are obliging. It is *ourselves* that we are being nice to, or doing a favor to. Admittedly, these things are not very simple. I am just as much confused about these as you are, maybe more. If you think you are not confused about these things, then you positively are. Listen to the prophets, and to the Jinas. No one else knows the truth, and that is the truth.

16. VEGETARIANISM.

Vegetarianism is probably the most well known, the most visible, and the most talked about part of Jainism. There is lot of confusion and misunderstanding about it. Vegetarianism is a direct offshoot of our reluctance to kill animals.

No religion really advocates the killing of animals. Even though meat-eating is almost a universal practice in the Western world, which is predominantly Christian, the Bible states in the First Commandment, 'Thou Shall Not Kill'. Apparently, its interpretation does not extend beyond the human beings.

We should avoid calling anyone else's behavior as 'Right' or 'Wrong'. If religion teaches us tolerance, that tolerance should extend to other religions as well. In general, people tend to do what they are born with, rather than what is 'Right', whatever that means.

If one is born into a meat-eating family, (s)he will eat meat, that is, be a non-vegetarian. One who is born in a vegetarian family will tend to be a vegetarian. Non-vegetarians do not avoid eating vegetables, while the vegetarians do avoid eating meat. Therefore, meat-eaters, and non-meat-eaters would have been a better way of saying it. Here also, convention prevails over logic.

Many non-vegetarians are leaning towards vegetarianism, and at the same time, many vegetarians are beginning to eat meat. I am a vegetarian, and I am also a physician. I have heard many arguments for and against eating or non-eating meat. It is obvious to me that in both camps there are healthy people, and there are weak people. Also, there are enough geniuses and enough fools on either side. Ultimately, it is a matter of individual preference based on family traditions, faith, and aesthetics.

Diet and food habits are integral parts of a culture, based on the climate, availability, and history. Even most of the vegetarians, as we know them, eat dairy products. There are some that don't. Imagine that from their point of view, we are as 'bad' as the non-vegetarians.

Take the other extreme example. There are cannibal tribes that eat human meat also. Even the staunchest non-vegetarian will be appalled at that idea. If we consider an average meat-eater, we see that (s)he may not like the idea of eating the meat of a dog, a horse, or a snake, or a rat, while in some parts of the world these are commonly eaten.

For a staunch Jain, eating any meat, fish, eggs, etc. is non-Jain, period. The fact is that many Jains today eat these. We cannot simply write them off. Being a Jain involves far more than just being a vegetarian. In a more practical sense, there is a whole spectrum of various levels of meat-eating. 'Thou shall not kill', when applied to life as a whole, indicates that we should move towards eating less and less meat, and should move from the cannibal end to the other end.

What is that end? It is certainly not what we call vegetarianism to-day. Vegetarians eat dairy products. As the argument goes, there is no killing or violence involved in that. You don't kill cows to get their milk. Maybe so, but the cows give milk under the same kind of circumstances as our mothers did, i.e., after delivering their babies. Imagine, if someone collected all the milk from our mothers, which was meant for us. Wouldn't you consider that as violence?

I should remind you, that we are not taking any sides here, and I am not telling you what you should do. We are just going over the facts as I know them. Maybe you know some more facts. Well, get them all together and think. Then you decide what is right for you. I am not trying to per-suade you.

Similar argument goes for eating eggs also. There is no life in some eggs. They are not fertilized, and even if you don't eat those eggs, no chicken is ever going to come out of them. Therefore, we are told, there is no violence in eating these. As we saw earlier, violence is not just killing in the obvious sense. Any kind of torture, imprisonment, terrorizing, or separating one from its (I am talking about animals) loved ones, also amounts to violence.

Twisting a doctrine or a principle
in order to violate it, is the
worst kind of violence.

In simple terms, once you start eating such infertile eggs, the psycho-logical barrier is broken. Then one day, by sheer mistake, you may eat other kinds of eggs. If you really wanted to do so, that's all well and good. But if you didn't want to eat eggs with life in them, then you goofed.

Whatever you decide to do, at least do it properly. Know and understand first.

All the meat packaging plants, slaughterhouses, poultry farms and fish hatcheries are violent establishments. They exist only to meet the demands. They exist because some of us eat meat, eggs, or fish. Whether we ourselves actually kill something or not is not relevant. As you recall, we are responsible for anything that is done for us, or with our blessings.

'What will happen to all these animals if we don't eat them? Wouldn't they eventually die anyway because of their increased population'? This argument is a mockery of mercy. Does it say that, 'We should eat these animals, so that they don't die'? These industries are called houses, farms, etc. where animals are bred and grown specifically for slaughter. So, when the demand goes down, fewer animals will be produced. The slaughter will never stop, because some people will always continue to eat meat.

If we stop eating meat, won't we prevent the owners of these farms from making a living, and won't we thereby commit violence? Everybody has a right to make a living, and we should never deprive anyone of his or her rights. Personally, I don't think that any plant owner or his family will starve to death, just because a few people will stop eating meat, or chicken, or whatever.

I don't watch much TV, but I am always astonished to see on it, an owner of a chicken business, proudly bragging about how good his chickens are, and that it is no wonder he sells almost three million of them everyday! When some of you need to eat only one chicken a day to fill your stomach, he has to kill three million of them to fill his! Is all that to make a living? Or, is he making a 'killing' (pardon the pun) every year in millions of dollars in profit?

You see? You can eat meat and other things out of concern for the animals (Lest they die), or out of a sense of justice (He has a right to make a living) or based on cool thinking (There is no life in that egg). It is very complicated. Do not think superficially. Things are not what they appear to be. The so called 'right action', without right knowledge and right understanding, is very dangerous. Therefore, Jinas say 'First Knowledge, then Mercy'.

*Before you act, first acquire
true knowledge and
true understanding.*

Otherwise, you will eat animals in order to keep them from dying, and will keep on eating them so that a chicken farmer will not die of starvation. There must be an easier way for all of us to live and make a reasonable living. There is a way, and Jinas have showed it to us.

It is the path involving the least violence. It is true that this planet is so full of life of all kinds, that it is nearly impossible to do anything without killing something. Vegetarians should not forget that the plants are also living things. Even if you choose not to eat vegetables and fruits, and decide to live only on air and water, these are full of life too.

Hindu scriptures tell us that 'Life is the Life of Life' or 'Living beings get their life from other living beings'. Sometimes this is used as an argument in favor of non-vegetarianism, that there is no other choice but to eat other living beings. The doctrine is wonderful, but like everything else, it has to be understood properly. We won't discuss it further, but what it really implies is that *we* exist thanks to others. We are under their obligation. 'Parasparopagraho Jivanam' (among lives, there is a mutual obligation), as Jainism says.

Children live off their parents. If children kill their parents, they themselves will die. Similarly, we all live off other forms of life. Now, if we indiscriminately destroy them, how long can we survive? If we keep on withdrawing money from the bank without depositing any, how long would the money last? Such questions are at the roots of the modern environmental concerns and ecological movements.

Avoiding waste, encouraging recycling, and protecting the environment from pollution, all have suddenly become urgent issues, because we have not heeded the word of the Jinas and other seers. We don't have to wait for our next birth to pay for our sins. They catch up with us right here, in this very life.

Once we know that our life depends on other lives, and that we are indebted to them, wouldn't we treat them as God, our conceptual life-giver? This is the reason that Asian Indians see God (Jainism is not against God, just to remind you) everywhere, viz., in water, in air, in fire, in forest, and in cows. The cow is sacred because our life is sacred. All life forms are sacred because our own life depends on them.

> *All forms of life are sacred*
> *because our own life*
> *depends on them.*

And we should never forget this. If we think our life is important, then we should be thankful to all life, including that in the plants, air, water or in the soil. Jainism advocates not even eating the plant life at least on a few days every month. It specifically advises against eating root vegetables like potatoes, onions, yams, carrots, radishes, and so on. Digging them out kills many earth organisms. Maybe, we shouldn't eat at all!

Yes, indeed! On some days of every month, Jains do fast. They don't eat at all, and some don't even drink water. They think about the word of the Jinas. Jains do not fast to kill themselves of starvation, but to thank other life forms for their own life, and to praise the Jinas for teaching them this.

All this is not meant to make you feel terribly guilty. There should be some fun and pleasure in our lives. If you do eat eggs, chicken, fish, or meat, you may not want to stop that for whatever reason. Try not to eat these at least on some day(s) of the week, or of the month. And don't forget to be thankful to all those animals who died, so that you could live. We build monuments for the soldiers who die for us. Let our life be a living monument to all those animals who died for us.

It would be hypocrisy to save plant life, but kill human beings. Tolerance to them and towards their thinking and beliefs is important. We already talked about the principle of Multiplicity of Viewpoints, and search for the truth. Now, let us continue with the rest of the Vratas.

(ii)   Truth.

The second Vrata is Truth, or **Satya.** Truth includes honesty to oneself and to others in all interactions of business, society, and relationships. Gandhiji applied this, and non-violence or Ahinsa (A = non, Hinsa = violence) in the field of national politics as well. These principles are not as easy to practice as it may seem at first. They require a great deal of commitment, determination and sacrifice. They are the ideals to strive for, and not the rules to enforce.

(iii)   Non-stealing (Asteya):

This involves not taking anything that does not belong to us, or which is not clearly given to us by its owner. Not to embezzle money entrusted to us is important. Practicing non-violence and truthfulness will lead to non-stealing almost automatically, but it is important to spell out everything.

(iv)   Celibacy (Brahmacharya):

Superficially, this vow refers to curtailing and refraining from sexual activity. It is known as the vow of Brahmacharya or the 'the quest of the highest one!'. An Atma in search of the Parmatma has to have some concentration of mind, and unity of purpose. The search for the Self is very demanding, and it requires a lot of strength.

In that journey one has to travel light. No excess or unnecessary baggage should be taken. A wandering mind constantly seeking out sexual gratification and adventures is not going to let anyone pursue anything else of value. The energy has to be focused and channeled properly.

We do not send a two year old child to school, because (s)he is still attached to the mother, and cannot live without her. Similarly, one who cannot live without his or her spouse for at least some time, is not going to achieve any lasting good for oneself or for society. Jainism does not deny the existence of sex drive. Nor does it condemn it, or call it evil. Shravaks and Shravikas are advised to limit their sexual relationships and desires to their spouses. Wooing of a prospective spouse is understandable.

The question is not whether sex is good or bad. It can be either. The question is that of our mission. The idea is to learn to control our desires and our mind. Marriage is not considered bad. A good spouse can actually help the partner in pursuit of spiritual bliss. Many Hindu ceremonies require both partners to take part. Jain celebrations do the same.

One should be faithful to, and content with one's spouse, without cheating, in mind, in speech, or in action. Not to lust in mind is not practical, but one should try to achieve that state. Cheating on one's spouse leads to a broken family, neglected children, subsequent alcoholism and drugs, and mental depression. Jealousy and mistrust can lead to violence and murder.

When both partners are ready, they can jointly take the fourth Vrata of celibacy for a limited time or for the rest of their lives. This is one step closer to becoming Sadhus and other aspired beings.

(v) Non-Hoarding (Aparigraha):

This means not accumulating wealth, possessions, power, etc. beyond the minimum that is absolutely essential. Personally, I am amazed by the enormous wisdom of the Jinas expressed in this Vrata. Charity is emphasized by many religions, wherein one is asked to give up a certain part, generally 6%, to the charity. Non-hoarding comes before that, and it goes way beyond that.

If a few people hoard a lot of things, they get rich, while others get poor. When a society is thus polarized, tension is created and the seeds of violence are sown. Charity has very little effect in easing that. On the other hand, non-hoarding prevents society from being polarized, and tension is prevented from building up. Now, even a little charity can go a long way.

Hoarding means taking over everything instead of sharing it. If one kid takes all the candies, the other children won't get any. It is hoarding, that creates the rich and the poor, or the 'haves' and 'have nots'. Such divisions of society are the root causes of many riots and revolutions, most of them violent. When deprived people get angry, they may try to attack our stores and us. All these problems are unnecessarily created by us, and they take us away from finding peace for ourselves.

In a practical sense, we never really 'need' dozens of shoes, suits, cars, houses, or boats. Once we get these, even if we never use them, we cannot give them up. Hoarding any item ties up our money also, which we could have used for other purpose. That makes us earn more money.

Most of us need many things, and may like to keep a little more on hand, just in case. At times, this gets out of hand, and we hoard more than what we can ever possibly use or need. This creates problems (of storage and security) for us, and it only ends up depriving others. You may know the story of the dog in the manger, in which a dog sits on a pile of grass and prevents the cows from eating it. The dog himself cannot eat it anyway.

What is most amazing to me is that Lord Mahavira thought about this Vrata 2500 years ago. Communism, Socialism, etc. are new ideas, and very recent ones. Mahavira went to the root cause of the problem of social unrest and suggested a solution.

Hoard not, and
hordes of your problems
will go away.

I have given only a superficial explanation here. If you think a little more deeply, you can see for yourselves, how hoarding can lead to stagnation and decay, waste of resources, and cause polluttion.

(vi) Other Vratas

These are the five major Vratas, although they are called 'minor' when compared to those for the monks. In all, there are twelve. It is not possible or necessary to discuss all of them here. The last four are called the 'Practice Vratas'. They are like exercises and should be done over and over again. One of these (the ninth) is called **Samayika.** We will talk about it in the Part II.

All these Vratas require constant alertness, introspection, vigilance and faith. They require a tremendous amount of self-control and discipline. An uncontrolled mind is attracted to every temptation. A well controlled mind permits us to stay on the right path. For that, we need the Three Gems.

17. THE THREE GEMS

We talked about the body, the Atma, and the role of Karma in perpetuating the cycle of reincarnation. We also talked about the grease and the soap that can affect Karma's attachment to the Atma. Then we talked about the Vratas to help us stay on the right path.

For most of you, these thoughts may be unfamiliar, but they are very old and are the precious possessions of the human race. I hope you are at least beginning to see your own 'selves' in a different way than you did before.

That's what knowledge does. It opens our eyes. It makes us look at things in a different light. Knowledge can free us from anxiety, worry and suffering. True knowledge makes many of our actions unnecessary. It gives us peace and salvation.

True knowledge is called **Samyag Gnyana** (true knowledge). It comes to us from the Jinas. The source of knowledge is important. If it comes to us from someone who is selfish, or who is a crook intent on taking away our money, or from someone who wants to gain our support, vote, etc., then the knowledge coming from that person can get us into trouble, and may land us in prison.

Samyag Gnyana is the first requirement for being free. Armed with that, we can hope to get true perception or **Samyag Darshana** (true vision). We can see things for what they are, and that we are not really happy, and that we are potentially no different than the great Jinas.

All the knowledge and perception of the world would do us no good unless we put it to good use - **Samyag Charitra** (proper conduct, right practice). Otherwise we remain like a doctor who never puts the stethoscope to his ears.

On the path to our freedom, these three - Samyag Gnyana, Samyag Darshana and Samyag Charitra, are the Three Gems (collectively called **'Ratnatrayi'** or a 'three-some of gems'). We need all three. They don't have to come one after the other. With practice, patience, and perseverance we can hope to get all three.

41

The twelve Vratas discussed earlier fall under the third gem, that of Samyag Charitra or right conduct. In acquiring these Three Gems, there are many things that can go wrong. Therefore at least once a year, every Shravak and Shravika (during the ritual of annual Pratikramana) goes through reciting a long but interesting list of transgressions. This 'Atichara Sutra' is reproduced in the Treasure chest in Part-III.

In these pages, I have tried to introduce you to Jainism as I understand it. There is no difference between us. We are all trying to reach the same destination. It is possible that I may have misunderstood the Jinas' word. You should try to find out for yourself. It is no use arguing about what is the truth, and what is more important. It is no use waiting for some god to right all the wrong things we do. Nor is it proper to blame destiny for all the ills that befall us.

Jinas have treated us as equal to themselves. We are responsible for all our actions. We are all equal, men, women, animals, plants and what not. If we have more power to do something or to think, let us help the others. When we hurt someone else, we hurt ourselves. Jinas have taught us how to change our ways, and have shown us the path that leads to the Jinas themselves.

Many have walked on that path. There was no point in telling you about Jinas and their glorious followers before you knew what the Jinas stood for. Now you know what the Jinas preached and practiced. They taught us to be kind and thankful to one another. You have tasted the fruits of their kindness and mercy upon us.

Now we are ready to know more about the Jinas and their followers who came before us. We should like to meet the people who gave us Jainism. We shall do that in Part III. There will be many stories in that part. But don't rush to that now. You probably would not be able to appreciate and enjoy those stories without reading the Part II first. Part I was the most difficult one. I compliment you on finishing it.

In Part II, we will look at Jainism as it is practiced today, and we will try to understand what we do, and why we do things. I will attempt to answer a few questions that usually come up, and to ease some of the doubts that I have heard from the young men and women I have met in America and elsewhere. Till then, Glory to the Great Jinas!

Jai Jinendra!

JAINISM   II

PRACTICE,   RITUALS   AND   RATIONALE

1. WHY DO WE PRACTICE RELIGION ?

In the first part, we looked at the basic principles of Jainism. Understanding these principles makes practicing the religion purposeful, meaningful, and more interesting. We do not go to the supermarket without knowing what we want to buy. Similarly, when we go to the temple, we should have some purpose in mind.

Practicing religion without understanding its principles is wasteful and dangerous. On the other hand, it is a great shame not to attempt to practice what we already know, and believe in. This latter part, 'believe in' is important.

You can listen to the message from the Jinas, from other prophets, or from your teachers, parents, friends, anyone. Generally, you do not want to do anything just because someone wants you to do it. Even if you do it out of fear, you may do only so much, and that also half heartedly.

On the other hand, if you agree with what is said, you may put your whole heart in doing it, and may produce better results. You have read about what the Jinas have said, and at present, you may or may not agree with some parts of it. Don't worry. Some of it may be my fault. I may not have said it properly. Often many important points may get lost in translation. Or, you may genuinely disagree.

You may choose not to practice the religion because you are not yet convinced. Well, no one should force you to. All we know is, that the Jinas were our well-wishers, and they themselves had nothing to gain by our practicing what they said. We may keep faith in their word and give it a try, even without completely agreeing with it. Understanding what is said is important; agreeing with it is good, but not absolutely necessary.

So many times it happens that we really do not grasp what is said until we practice it. A description of the Statue of Liberty or of the Taj Mahal may not make you want to go there, but once you do go, you may be thankful, and glad that you did. You may even understand and appreciate better, the description you read at first, and any reservations and disagreements that you may have had can disappear.

This kind of trust, to follow someone or something even when we are not sure, or convinced, is called 'faith'. It is very essential in the practice of religion. Faith means that you trust the Jinas and their word because you 'know' that they are on your side.

Science and logic depend upon proof and understanding. Religion is not a science in the usual sense, and a scientific proof of religious principles is not possible. When it is, it becomes science. Even a scientist recognizes that (s)he is not perfect and that there is truth and knowledge beyond what is known. This is his or her faith.

When we are sick, we trust a physician. When we are lost, we trust the gas station attendant. When we are puzzled and confused in matters of life and spirit, we should have faith in the Jinas, and in their word.

In the United States, when we want to start jogging, or playing tennis, first of all we get the appropriate dress and shoes, and then go to a track or to a tennis court. In practicing religion there are special tools, dresses, and places also, but there is one big difference. We can practice religion without any special equipment. Only ourselves and our faith will be enough.

When you think about religion, you may think about temples, prayers, worships, fasting, monks, nuns, some chanting, some Sanskrit writings, and some unfamiliar and at times weird-looking pictures. All these are necessary, and yet only the apparent parts of religion. The real religion is inside your heart and soul, between you and the Jinas.

We are like a radio or a television set, and the Jinas are like the radio or TV station from where the signals are coming. We have to keep a good antenna pointed in the proper direction. We have to avoid interference from overhead electric wires, microwaves, nearby skyscrapers, passing airplanes, etc. If there are mountains or elevated electric train tracks nearby, we cannot receive the signals well. We need a good receiver, and non-interfering surroundings.

We can also compare ourselves with a violin or a piano. We should be in tune to play the music properly. One needs a good orchestra and a good auditorium for one to experience good music.

Let us prepare ourselves first. We have to prepare our body and our mind. Although body is transient, and is going to die, we should not despise it. It is a tool to do good deeds. It is a house in which the Atma lives. Since the Atma is the same as that of the Jinas, our body should be treated like a temple.

The body should be kept healthy, with good food, exercise, rest, and medical help as needed. An ill or weak body can make one very selfish, and unfit to help others. Too much or too little or the wrong kind of food, exercise or rest are not desirable either.

The body should not be pampered. After all, it is only a tool, or a vehicle. We cannot just keep on waxing our car, we have to go somewhere. A pampered body, with too many clothes, perfumes, make-up, etc. is going to become very demanding, and it would not leave us time for anything else.

In our everyday life, and especially in religious rituals, we need a body that can move swiftly, can remain steady for a long time, is free from wounds, pus, or bad odors.

Body carries our five sense organs, viz., eyes, ears, tongue, nose and skin. These are the organs of sight, smell, sound, taste, and touch, respectively, as you know so well. All of them like good things, and they despise the bad ones. They keep us chasing the good, and new, and different sights, sounds, tastes, etc. all the time.

These sense organs are under the control of our mind. As long as the mind keeps on demanding better and better, and more and more sights, sounds, and fragrances, our body will never be able to sit down and listen or do anything else.

We cannot sit steadily unless our mind is calm. The mind is like a monkey. It is very restless. It jumps from one thing to another. It makes us run after one thing or other, and like a spoiled child, it tires us out. It wants more and more. It is never satisfied. You give more, and it wants still more. But, if you give less, it can learn to live with less, and still less.

The mind can be disciplined.
A monkey can be tamed
and trained.

Instead of our dancing to its tunes, we can make it dance to ours. Once our mind is calmed down, and the body settles down, we are ready to act on the Jina's word, or at least to listen to it. We can focus our energy into our task at hand, rather than wasting it on trivialities. Unless we learn to control our senses, we will be slaves of our monkey-mind.

This is important in our everyday life also. If we can train our mind not to wander, and thus make our body less restless, we can do our study or other work more efficiently. Even if you never become a religious person, with these habits you can be a successful person.

Even the slightest practice of religion
gives big rewards.

The mind always wants to do something. We can tell it to do what we want. So, we have to withdraw it from its wanderings, then channel it into the Jina's word or into our studies, or other work.

Recognize that our body is
a tool for doing good things. It is a temple of our Atma
which is no different from that of the Jinas.

Recognize also that our mind is
like a monkey, and is like a spoiled brat.
However, it has a lot of energy which can be
put to some good use.

We always thought that 'we' meant either our body, or our mind. Our language reflects this too. 'We did this', or 'We will come', or 'We will do what we want to do', or 'Do what pleases you', and so on. Once we understand this, we can proceed to control our mind. We have never tried to do this before. We should make our mind and our body work towards what is good for the Atma, just as the courts, the Senate, and the President, all work to do what is good for the Nation.

2. PRACTICAL WAYS
TO CONTROL THE MIND

The mind runs towards everything it notices. Therefore, the biggest hurdle in controlling it is the innumerable distractions in our daily lives. We can stop many of these, and if we cannot, 'We' should just tell the body to ignore what the mind says. This is the first step in conquering oneself. We have to break our false or make-believe self so that the real one can come out, just as a chicken breaks through the egg and looks up.

'We' are the boss.

If it is possible, move away from distractions. This is easier than trying to control them. Go to a quiet place, away from all the noise and the usual attachments of the room, our clothes, our shoes, 'our' this or that, the sound of our stereo, and the smell of the goodies from the kitchen. School is one place, the library is another, a temple is still another. There are many more.

We cannot always do that. Therefore wake up before everyone else does, or stay up later. Turn the TV and the radio off. Give your stereo some rest. Put the phone off the hook, if that is acceptable, or have someone else answer it for you. Do not chew gum or eat candy.

At first, you won't like this. Your mind and body will rebel the way you rebel when your parents ground you. Once you learn to ground yourself, you will have the same power as your parents have. Yes, this is hard, but being the boss is never easy. It is a major responsibility.

The more you control yourself,
the freer you will be from
the outside authorities.

Every big journey consists of many small steps. You can do this 'controlling' gradually, one thing at a time, a little bit at a time. Jainism shows you many ways to do this. For example, you may give up your favorite candy for a day, a week, a month, or until after you have finished this book.

You may decide not to eat anything for an hour or two after you wake up, or until after sunrise, or you may decide to stop eating at sunset.

If you do eat meat or chicken, or drink alcohol, you may choose not to, at least during the holy days of Paryushana, or maybe, not to eat these on the weekends, or whatever. There are many kinds of vows, small and big that one can take. Yes, you can start with the silliest ones like 'I would not kill a hippopotamus'. You do this because your mind is still a monkey. It is still controlling you. It does not want you to control it, and you are doing it a favor by listening to it, while hurting yourself.

Once you control your body and mind, you have to make them do what you intended in the first place. If you leave them just sitting there, they get bored, and start looking for mischief. You can do your home-work, or read something, or think about what you have read. Do not just think about which new record album or which new dress you want to buy for your birthday. If you do that, you are giving your mind a free reign.

We have never bothered to think about our true self. We have worried too much, and for too long about our bodies and our minds, and in doing so, surrendered our true self to them. We have to find and dig out our true 'Self'.

Our mind just reaches out everywhere to find what it likes and what pleases it. Once we show the mind that pleasantaries do not really make us happy, it calms down. At times, the mind runs towards alcohol, tobacco, caffeine and harder drugs like cocaine to make it feel good. It is trying to find peace, but we have to show it the way.

As long as we are lost,
we cannot be at peace.

Alcohol and other drugs make us forget our real selves. But that has been our problem all along. We have forgotten ourselves, and hence we are not happy. Alcohol and other drugs will not restore our peace. When religion forbids such things, it is not just to torture us, but to save us from deep trouble.

'But why didn't you say so?' you may wonder. Well, the Jinas have been telling us that all along. We never had time to listen to them. We were too busy pampering our body and catering to our mind. We have been slaves to our pleasures and desires. We do not even know that we are slaves and that we are not happy.

As we go further, we will talk about many rituals to practice religion. The purpose behind all these rituals is to achieve self-control. If the rituals are carried out without any understanding, it can hurt, and even bind us further.

What we are discussing now, is what lies behind all the rituals, i.e., to gain self-control. When we talk about them, we will not discuss all this again. Rituals without anything behind them are hollow, like sleep-walking. They are like a handshake without any warmth, or a kiss without any love, or like a check without a bank balance. It is a waste of time and a mockery of religion and of the Jinas.

Many rituals are symbolic gestures, like sending flowers to a loved one. But there are some gestures that are direct, and straight forward. They are the do's and don'ts of our daily life. They are the code of behavior of a Shravak, and a Shravika. This code of behavior is called 'Achara' (Chara = to walk, to move about), i.e., how we should go about, in our everyday business.

3. CODE OF CONDUCT 'ACHARA'

If you have read this book well so far, you yourselves can practically write this chapter. I am not quoting all this from a book, but writing it based on common sense, and on what we have already discussed. We can enumerate what to do. Out of necessity, this is a superficial and sketchy summary. Once you get into this, there are detailed descriptions available.

(A) FOR ONE'S OWN SELF

(i)   Read, listen, think about, and practice the Jina's word.
(ii)   Practice self control, non-violence, tolerance, and
(iii) Avoid waste, cheating, stealing; avoid vices, and drugs.
(iv)   Participate in the activities of the Sangha, and in its rituals. Provide money and other help.
(v)   Spread the Jina's word to your children, and to others if they specifically ask for it.
(vi)   Keep your body healthy, but do not pamper it.
(vii) Meet all your needs, but keep your wants to a minimum. Don't be greedy, angry or vengeful.

(B) TOWARDS THE FAMILY

(i)   Be kind, loving, respectful, and nurturing.
(ii)   Discuss the Jina's word with them, and encourage its practice, first by your own example, then by providing encouragement, good environment and support.
(iii) Teach them what constitutes good conduct at home, at the temple, and at the Sangha functions.
(iv)   Do not disturb in, interfere with, or laugh at their religious practice.

(C) WITH OTHER JAINS

(i)   Treat them like your family.

(ii) Learn how to behave with the monks and nuns. Provide for their food, lodging, and other needs, and for continuing their religious practice and preaching.

(iii) Hold religious festivals, processions, and other observances to involve the whole Sangha.

(iv) Provide facilities for practicing religious rituals, especially for those requiring special food, water and equipment.

(v)   Encourage such practices by felicitations, and ceremonies, and by distributing gifts to encourage others, especially children.

(D) WITH NON-JAINS

(i)   Be tolerant. Respect and try to understand their religions. Do not argue over which is better. Treat their religion as yours.

(ii) Do not give up your religion just because another religion appears easier or more rewarding.

(iii) Cooperate with them to spread the good word. See the common ground, and patch up the differences.

(iv) Do not try to convert them to Jainism, but do tell them about it if they ask. Give proper answers. If you cannot, ask someone to help you. Do not try to sell Jainism, nor use it to provide entertainment.

(v)   Do not feel compelled to explain everything you do. It is your personal matter.

(vi) Be especially tolerant to those who believe neither in religion, nor in any God.

(E) WITH OTHER THINGS AND CREATURES

(i)   As a Sangha, or as a religious group, do not get involved in political activities. As an individual, by all means try to further the principles. Do not impose your views on others. That is violence.

(ii) Take good care of your pet animals, or your work-horses. Do not destroy wildlife. Do not kill every non-human moving thing you see. Pick-up a dying earthworm from the dry, hot asphalt and put it on the moist, shaded soil. Both of you will feel better.

53

Remember, you are not doing any of this to impress others, to please the Jinas, or as a favour to those you deal with, or to get anything in return. You do this because you think it is the right thing to do, you like to do it, and doing it makes you feel at peace with yourself. Well, that's what religion is all about.

Good conduct is called **Achara.** Lack of it is called **Anachara.** In practicing the Achara, you may do it wrongly, improperly, inadequately, grudgingly, or disrespectfully. These transgressions are called **Aticharas.** Later on, in the Treasure Chest, we will look at some Aticharas, so that you can have a more practical idea about conduct in our daily lives.

4. EFFORT AND PERSEVERANCE

Once we know the right things and understand them, we attempt to practice what we learn, and practice it the right way. If there are transgressions or mistakes, (Atichara) we should acknowledge that and try to correct them. True knowledge and true understanding are not enough for proper implementation. Constant effort (**Virya**) and perseverance (**Tapa**) are also required. Virya means striving and exerting prowess. It means putting oneself to the task at hand. Tapa means suffering for it. Tapa literally means 'to heat up'.

A blacksmith heats up the piece of iron he is working on, and then hammers it into the desired shape. The same example applies to one's own character. One has to go through a lot, to develop and shape oneself. George Washington and his soldiers did that at Valley Forge, but a forge (blacksmith's work place, with fire) it was, incidentally.

Character-building involves controlling the mind and the body. The mind operates through the body and the sense organs. To control the mind from being more and more demanding, we should pamper the body less and less. The Jinas took that to the extreme, by depriving the body of food, shelter, clothing, and the pleasures of the senses.

As long as we are slaves of our minds, and its desires for the pleasures of the senses, we cannot be free. The Jinas' forging, or Tapa, is awe-inspiring. They took the human body to its limits of tolerance.

They did not wait for the mind to mellow on its own. They worked on that too, at the same time. To one who does not understand this, all this may sound like self-torture, but the idea is to 'kill' (not literally) our false self to bring out the true one; to make the mind withdraw from everything, including concern for its own life and existence, and to join it with the supreme and the freed beings - the Siddhas. Even for the mundane, everyday success, self control is essential.

The mind is like a despotic prince or king, used to having things its own way, taking over our body, and tarnishing our soul. When finally, the mind and body are totally changed and joined in the service of ourselves and of the Siddhas, our soul shines through, and that is the ultimate knowledge, Kevala Gnyana. We cannot describe it further.

We are no way near there, and are not ready or even worthy to try all that. But we can do something too. Even if we cannot throw away the mind's tyranny totally and permanently, there is no reason to accept it wholly and forever either. We can do just enough to remind us that we are the masters. We can at least admire what the Jinas did, and remind us that we can do it too.

Doing Tapa is not a public performance. It is a private study and an experiment. It is like the basic training in a boot camp that soldiers go through. They have to fight for the freedom of the country, but we have to fight for our own freedom. Let us look at some of the Tapas of the body and of the mind. Every little bit helps. No Tapa is too small.

5. TRAINING THE BODY AND THE MIND

When a revolution to overthrow a government is to take place, the army is first taken into confidence, so that it refuses to obey official orders and starts obeying the orders from the revolutionary junta (a committee). The official government becomes powerless and then collapses. Our body is our army, and we should put it in the service of our Atma (soul), rather than of our mind.

Ours is a bloodless revolution. We go slowly but surely. We have to teach the body where its real interest lies. The body is always under pressure from the mind. So how do we begin? First, we must have faith in the Jinas and have confidence in ourselves. We should remember what we are trying to achieve, and why. We are not training for the Olympics or for a place in the Guinness' Book of World Records. We may always start with small vows.

Almost all the vows discussed in this section are about food; either to eat less, eat later, not eat at all, or make our food relatively taste free but nutritious. Also, the frequency and extent of these Vratas can be increased as tolerance develops. It is always better to try to do a little more than what feels comfortable.

A. PHYSICAL TAPAS

1. Chauvihara. The simplest are the eating restrictions in the morning and the evening, that is, not eating before sunrise or after sunset. Not eating after sundown is called Chauvihara. Literally it means all 'four kinds' of food that one stops eating at sundown. The four kinds are (i) food, (ii) drink, (iii) chewing gum, etc., and (iv) mouth fresheners and so on. This is the easiest Tapa to do, and many Shravaks and Shravikas do it all their lives as a routine. It is also done as part of any fasting you do.

Chauvihara involves not putting anything in your mouth, including a tooth brush or tooth paste after sundown, through the night, until 48 minutes after sunrise the next day. It is better to begin the Chauvihara a few minutes before sunset, to make sure there is no overlap. Remember, no one is making you do this. You choose to do it on your own, so do it well.

2. Navakarashi. This involves not eating anything until 48 minutes after sunrise. It can also be done without doing a Chauvihara the night before, but after a Chauvihara, a Navakarashi should always be done the next morning. It is also done after any partial or total fast. The way to conclude Navakarashi is to sit down at the proper time, 'count' or recite the Navakara Mantra three times, then rinse the mouth and then brush.

Note that Chauvihara starts at sunset, while Navakarashi starts 48 minutes after sunrise. The reason being, after sunset, light rapidly fades off, but it takes some time after sunrise for the day to brighten. We will not describe this or other rituals completely. They should be learned from parents, teachers, or from special books. Eating can be delayed for longer periods also, and these vows go by different names.

In all the Tapas, it is important
to take a pledge to do so
beforehand

Taking a pledge itself gives you some extra power. It is like taking an oath, or like the Pledge of Allegiance to the Flag. The pledges for various Tapas are prescribed in the holy books. Any senior member of the family or a Guru can administer that. One can read it from a book as well.

The pledge is called a **Pachchakhana** ('to state against'), because it proclaims your intention of not doing something for a certain time. Navakarashi, Chauvihara, and other Tapas to be discussed, all require us to take a Pachchakhana.

3. Partial Fasting. Once we can do Chauvihara and Navakarashi, we can progress to limit our eating to only twice a day, called a ***Besanun*** (from Be = two, Asana = to sit), or eating only once, called an ***Ekasanun*** (Eka = one). This is how it works. If you are to do any of these tomorrow, you start with a Chauvihara tonight, do the Ekasanun or Besanun tomorrow, do Chauvihara tomorrow also, and end with a Navakarashi the day after tomorrow.

The concluding vow of any partial or total fast or even Chauvihara or Navakarashi, is called a **'Paranun'** meaning 'conclusion'. After this we may start eating again. One warming. It can be extremely dangerous to eat too much or even the usual breakfast on an empty stomach. Go slowly. Your stomach has already learned to live with less.

You have succeeded. Your mind has not learned yet, so it is getting greedy. Believe me, Paranun can be the most difficult part of the Tapa. Paranun is not your goal or destination. It is only a level walk during climbing a mountain, before the next ascent.

Even after you go back to your regular business, and to snacking in front of the TV, you will notice that you have changed. You will find that now the urge to eat is not as pressing or as overwhelming as it was before. The real boss is back, and is taking charge again.

Ayambil is an Ekasanun, but no seasonings or spices are added to food. Ghee (clarified butter), oil, raw salt, sugar, dairy products, honey, etc. are avoided. Mostly boiled food is eaten. This Tapa helps us to learn to control our taste-buds. An Ayambil can be done on any day, but twice a year there are special 9-day periods during which 1-9 successive Ayambils can be done.

4. Total Fasting. This is not necessarily more difficult than the partial fasts discussed earlier. To some, not eating at all is easier than eating once or twice a day. Total fasting gives you total freedom from the kitchen and the shopping, so that now you have all the time in the world to think and read about yourself, and about the Jinas.

A fast is called *'Upavasa'* (with 'U' as in Put. 'Upa-' means 'sub-'; Vasa means 'to stay'). Just as a suburbanite lives next to a city (urban area), the people doing an Upavasa live next to the Jinas, or in the company of the Jina's word. Upavasa does not mean just fasting. It means freeing yourself from other things and then sitting down with the Jinas.

While fasting, if all you think about is eating, or about the Paranun to come the next morning, or if you go about your everyday business as usual, or worse, if you go to a movie house or a casino to kill time, or if you just watch TV, you are not doing an Upavasa. You are just torturing yourself. The idea is to withdraw from these things, and to approach the Jinas. We cannot always take days off from school or from our work, but the point is, our thoughts have to change.

During the Tapa one should go to the temple, to religious lectures, or should just stay home and read religious books or do other religious activities. This is not an extra burden. This is the reason to do the fast. If you go to school, you study. You don't say, 'It is bad enough going to school, but on top of that *study* ? How awful!' If you think so, you might as well not go to school.

Before we leave the physical Tapa, let me say one more word. Tapas are not for convenience, nor for sheer fun. Since it is not compulsory to do any Tapa and in as much as there are Tapas of varying severity to suit our varying capacities, there is no need to water them down so that we can reach higher.

On the day of any partial or total fast, you are not supposed to brush your teeth. This creates a lot of resentment in the (monkey) minds of us, the modern people. Some do not mind fasting but would insist on brushing their teeth. It is your vow, and you can decide what you do, but try to understand.

How does fasting take you near the Jinas? You don't have to cook or do the dishes, so you won't have to shop. You feel weak, so you are not likely to replace the roof of your house either. You cannot go to a party, or for a pizza. You do not brush your teeth either.

Brushing your teeth raises your expectations for a breakfast, making fasting more difficult. It restores your appetite for food, and also for the opposite sex. The former is forbidden, and the latter is not prudent. Not brushing saves you from both of these. There are ways to clean your teeth with boiled water.

During an Ekasanun, a Besanun, an Ayambil, or an Upavasa, we use boiled (and then cooled) water. Some do Upavasa without taking any water. Some do 2-3 or even eight consecutive Upavasas. I have heard of 56 Upavasas. But again, we are not trying to break any records.

Tapas help us in
joining our minds to the Jinas.
We may be able to do this without any Tapas at all,
merely by filling our minds
with good thoughts.

B. MENTAL TAPAS :

Our mind is an invisible monkey so we cannot literally tie it down. We know it is very restless, proud, arrogant, and self-centered. Like a child, it takes everything in. We can retrain it to make it think good thoughts, to be humble and modest, make it think of others around us who may need help, and finally, to fill it with the word of the Jinas. There are several mental Tapas to help us do that.

1. Repentance: It means feeling and saying 'I am sorry!' It is very important, and is not an automatic, verbal process. A lot more is involved. First, one has to recognize one's mistake, especially in dealing with others. This requires constantly looking over one's own thoughts and actions. Even then mistakes can happen. When a mistake is recognized, one gets the feeling, 'My God! Did I do that! Look at all the suffering I caused. No wonder he was so upset. How terrible! And he was even trying to help me!....'

Like this, there can be layers and layers of true repentance. There are instances recorded in the scriptures that repentance by itself has taken people all the way to Kevala Gnyana or the state of becoming an Arihanta. Repentance is not a proclamation, it is a state of mind. 'Holy tears of repentance can wash out any sin', to paraphrase the Gujarati poet 'Kalapi'.

*Repentance by itself
can take one
all the way to Kevala Gnyana.*

The mind can go from the lowermost level to the highest (there are fourteen main levels, called 'Virtue-Stations') just by sincere repentance. Therefore, it is the Atma's most effective Tapa. This is not as easy as it may seem. Not every mind is capable of doing this. Our pride, arrogance, and ignorance come in the way. There are ways to overcome these also.

2. Humility and Modesty: It is hard to be proud or arrogant when you are kneeling or bowing down or sitting on a lower seat. This is what you do with your parents, elders, teachers, monks and the Jinas. Joining two hands in prayer does the same thing.

3. Service and Charity: When we see the suffering of others, we realize that we are not really in such bad shape. When we help others, we forget our own worries. Our monks, nuns, Shravaks, Shravikas, temples, and monasteries need our help. Plus, there are others. There are birds, animals, and the environment. They need our help. They are doing a great deal for us, so it is only natural that we should keep them well.

Jainism places a strong emphasis on donating knowledge – teaching someone, distributing books, giving tuition fees for college, building schools and colleges and libraries, protecting our manuscripts, encouraging and supporting research into the old texts, and so on.

4. Self-study: This is called *Svadhyaya* (Sva = self, Adhyaya = study). This involves sitting down quietly and reading or meditating (thinking) upon the scriptures (holy books). This removes our arrogance, and teaches us that there are people greater than ourselves.

5. Meditation (Dhyana): In its simplest from, Dhyana is the practice of making the mind thought-free. The popular culture in America talks a great deal about Yoga and Meditation. There are books and books written on this subject, but it is better discussed with a teacher. There are many claims made about various powers that meditation and Yoga can generate. These powers do not come from outside. They are your own powers, which are unleashed.

One example will make this point clear. Once someone praised Michaelangelo's sculpture showing a beautiful woman's figure. 'How did you create her?' the visitor asked. 'I didn't create her. She was in there. I removed everything else, so she came out' responded the sculptor.

That's the knowledge and the power that the Jinas had. All other power and knowledge only place the Atma in further bondage. True knowledge is to know one-self, and the real power is the self-control.

> *True knowledge is*
> *knowing one's self, and*
> *real power is self-control.*

6. Chanting the Lord's name: This is called 'Kayotsarga' (Kaya = body, Utsarga = flushing through, a catharsis). We are supposed to sit in meditation, and pray to the Jinas by saying 'Namo Arihantanam...' etc. over and over again. This can go on from once or twice, to innumerable times over hours. The purpose of the Kayotsarga is to remind ourselves that we are not the body, but we are the soul, and are basically not different from the Jinas.

5. SAMAYIKA

There is a way to combine all the Tapas of the mind, and it is fairly easy and interesting for a beginner. It is called **Samayika.** Samayika and the Navakara Mantra (Namo Arihantanam....Padhamam Havai Mangalam) are two things in Jainism that you can write about forever, and yet never finish it. The Navakara is used for chanting the Lord's name, and it is present in everything you do in Jainism.

Samayika is like a gym period for the mind, and to some extent for the body too. In the gym, you generally jump around, while in Samayika you learn to sit still and keep your mind still. It is a ritual to condition the body and the mind.

'Sam' (pronounced here as 'some') means 'an equal, stable, calm attitude', while 'Ay' (rhymes with 'why') means 'to come'. Samayika ('Sam' is pronounced here, in Samayika, as in 'palm') is a practice which enables us to acquire and maintain a calm, quiet attitude to facilitate thinking about the Jina's word.

Samayika can be done in one's home. We will not describe it in great detail here. It is easy to learn and is preferably done in front of a Guru (teacher). It takes less than an hour. Entering it and leaving it takes a few minutes. The actual Samayika is for 48 minutes (= two Ghadis, or = one Muhurat).

These 48 minutes are a quiet period, to read scriptures, to pray, to chant, and to discuss religious principles (minimal talking is allowed). During the Samayika, you cannot eat, drink, get up, or touch a member of the opposite sex.

No use of electricity is permitted either. So you have no lights, and of course no television, radio, or tape player (not even battery operated, that's electric too). Upto three Samayikas can be done in a row. Samayika is a good way to build stamina, memory, and to develop concentration.

During the Samayika, you are trying to withdraw your mind from transient things. Therefore, no house work or business work can be discussed or done during the Samayika. If you do talk, do not discuss day to day things, do not gossip, and do not discuss the world news. You are in a meeting with the Jinas, and you cannot be disturbed.

Samayika teaches you mind control, modesty (you respect your Guru), repentance (in the process of entering a Samayika, you apologize for any incidental violence you committed on that day), and you do Svadhyaya, Meditation, and Kayotsarga. At the same time you prevent the body from seeking out pleasures.

You should not look around too much, and should try not to pay attention to any sounds. Ideally you should be in a quiet place. If no such place can be found in the home, then one should go to a monastery. While in Samayika, you are a monk. And the monks are considered to be always in the Samayika. Just as the President of the United States is always on duty.

6. PRATIKRAMANA

One can also do some prescribed actions during the Samayika. Instead of doing the religious reading, meditation, or chanting either with the help of beads or without, one can follow a structured path, which includes all of the above. This kind of Samayika is called a Pratikramana.

Pratikramana means 'to withdraw', or to do the opposite of our nature as dictated to by our mind. (Prati = opposite, Kru = to do). When you fight against your enemies, it is called Pratikara. With Pratikramana, we want to charge against our internal enemies viz., desire, anger, greed, attachments, likes, dislikes, and so on.

The morning Pratikramana is called **Rai** (pertaining to the night, which is 'Ratri' in Sanskrit) Pratikramana, and the evening one is called **Devasi** (pertaining to the day, called 'Divas' in Sanskrit) Pratikramana. The Rai Pratikramana goes over the sins, lapses, and transgressions that may have occurred during the night, and gets the day off to a good start. The Devasi Pratikramana puts us to sleep with a quiet mind, filled with holy, pleasant and uplifting thoughts.

This business of always apologizing may not appeal to all of us. Time maybe a factor too. We can do one or the other Pratikramana, if not daily, maybe every few days or maybe during the religious days. When a Pratikramana is done on the fourteenth or the twenty eighth day of the month, it is called **Pakshika** Pratikramana ('Paksha' means a fortnight; literally, one of the two 'parts' of a lunar month). The one that is done on a three-times-a-year schedule (you may do one or more of these in a year) is called **Chaumasi** Pratikramana (Chau = four, remember 'Chauvihara? Masa = a month).

During the year, you should do at least one Pratikramana, only on the last of the religious days. It is called **Samvatsari** Pratikramana. Samvatsara means 'a year'. The five Pratikramanas are named according to the time when they are done, and not only according to the frequency with which you do them.

The Pakshika, Chaumasi and Samvatsari are all modifications of the Devasi Pratikramana, and hence they are done in the evening. The Rai and the Devasi Pratikramanas take about an hour each, while the other three take 1.5 to 2.5 hours, or more depending upon how well they are done. It is a good idea to do at least a Samvatsari Pratikramana, but it is better to do Devasi Pratikramana once or twice in the few days before the big one, just to warm up.

All Pratikramanas and the Samayika require you to say (in your mind) the Navakara Mantra several times, anywhere from one to sixteen times in the daily Pratikramanas, and upto 161 times at once during the Samvatsari Pratikramana. You should learn the Navakara Mantra and do that part well. If you cannot follow the rest of the Pratikramana, you can continue to 'count' (that is, recite it in your mind, you don't have to count them aloud) the Navakara all the time, instead of letting your eyes and thoughts wander.

Suppose you do only one Pratikramana in a year, and you want to do it today. In the morning you do the Rai Pratikramana. If you choose to do it in the evening, then it can be the Devasi, the Pakshika, the Chaumasi, or the Samvatsari Pratikramana depending upon what day of the year it is. A Samayika you can always do, at any time and on any day but generally not between 10 at night and 5 in the morning.

The instructions to do Samayika, Pratikramana or almost anything else are called '**Vidhi**' (a recipe). The Vidhi tells you in what order you do what, when you should count the Navakara Mantra, and so on. These Vidhis are easily available in many books. To put them on an audio or video cassette is not a good idea, since you are not supposed to use any appliances during these rituals. One's conduct during the Pratikramanas is supposed to be the same as that during a Samayika.

If you want to make such tapes for demonstration purpose or as a memory aid, in my personal opinion (which very few may share) you can do that for your own use. It is better than listening to or watching some other tapes. You cannot under any circumstances do a Pratikramana with a tape. Such a tape, if it is made, should be treated like a religious book, as a sacred treasure, and it must be treated with utmost care and respect.

We talked about the Navakara Mantra and the Atichara Sutra. There are many more Sutras. The Pratikramana Vidhi consists of many such Sutras. They are very interesting. Once you understand their meaning, you can get more out of the Pratikramanas. To begin with, you should know the purpose of the Sutras.

The Samayika requires about ten Sutras, but even if you do not know these, someone can help you into and out of the Samayika. It takes a couple of minutes each time. The two daily Pratikramanas require additional 15-20 Sutras, and the other three require another 15-20 Sutras. Many of these are prayers, some are narrative, some others are excellent poems, and some are quite lyrical. All are worthwhile.

You can memorize these even without understanding at first. We did it that way. You only train your memory by doing so. You can get into the meaning gradually. We will look at a sample of a few Sutras later on, in the Treasure Chest in Part III.

The Navakara is present everywhere. The Atichara Sutra is said during the Pakshika, Chaumasi, and Samvatsari Pratikramanas. The daily ones have mini versions of the Atichara Sutra. The morning Pratikramana has one Sutra that lists all the known major temples and places of pilgrimage. Another one lists all the great Jain people, historical or fictional. There are many men and women in it, and their names taken in the morning can really give your day a good start.

PARTS OF A PRATIKRAMANA

The Pratikramanas are generally in six parts called the **Avashyaka** ('necessary'). You already know most of them.

1. The first Avashyaka is **Samayika**. All Pratikramanas begin and end with the Samayika.
2. The second Avashyaka is **Chauvisaththo** or paying respect to the Tirthankaras.
3. The third is **Vandana** or paying respect to the Guru.
4. The fourth is the **Pratikramana** itself, which involves withdrawing from all sins and coming back to good thoughts.
5. The fifth is **Kayotsarga**. That is, counting the Navakara Mantra as recommended in the Vidhi.
6. The sixth is **Pachchkhana**. The Rai Pratikramana is always followed by a Navakarashi. The Devasi and other Pratikramanas are followed by a Chauvihara. You may keep the option of taking medicine and water if you are in ill health.

7. MEETING THE SANGHA –
AN UPASHRAYA

Just to orient you once again, we are talking about practicing Jainism in order to achieve control over ourselves as the Jinas did. Towards this end, we went over what our Achara (conduct) should be like. To improve our conduct, we should train our body with various Tapas, including fasting, and should train our mind with repentance, courtesy, service, charity and so on.

To train the mind, we do Samayika and Pratikramana. These can be done at home, but preferably they should be done in the presence of a Guru, who is generally an Acharya (the leader of the monks). Any Vidhi done in the presence of others is more likely to be proper than the one done alone.

Monks live in a monastery called an Upashraya (Up = substitute, ancillary, Ashraya = a shelter). For monks, their real shelter is the Jinas and their teachings. Monks do not have their own home or house, so they live in an Upashraya provided by the Shravaks and Shravikas, and generally located next to a temple. Many of the rituals like Samayika, etc. mentioned thus far, can be done in the Upashraya also.

An Upashraya is a big, but simple and austere place with one or more halls, and sometimes with a few small rooms. It is dimly lit and the lights are not used during the Pratikramanas or whenever monks are present. In the main hall, which is used for the **Vyakhyana** (a lecture) by the Acharya or the next available monk, there is a big, flat wooden bench (called a '**Pata**', with the first 'a' as in Last) on which the Acharya sits. There are smaller and lower benches for other monks.

Shravaks and Shravikas sit on the bare floor, in separate sections. Shravaks sit in front and on the right hand side of the lecturer while Shravikas sit on the left hand side of the lecturer. Children can sit on either side, but boys sit with their fathers, and girls with their mothers. This is because some do Samayika there, and during a Samayika, one is not supposed to touch a member of the opposite sex.

Jainism does not treat women as either inferior or bad. Women do everything that men do. There have been many women Siddhas, Arihantas, and at least one Tirthankara too. However, Sadhvis generally do not deliver the main lecture (Vyakhyana), nor do they preside over the Pratikramana if a male Acharya is present. They do deliver the afternoon lectures, and preside over the Pratikramana if only women are present. This may be due to the cultural deference to men, but nuns are not considered inferior in any way.

When the Acharya delivers the Vyakhyana or when he presides over a Pratikramana, he symbolically puts his own Guru (teacher) in front of him on a small stand holding a few holy objects. At home, Shravaks and Shravikas put a book on a stand and establish that as the Acharya. This symbolic Guru is called a **Sthapanacharya** (established Acharya). In the presence of a real Guru (a monk) we do not need that.

Shravaks and Shravikas can go and live in the Upashraya for a few days as monks and nuns, after taking the appropriate vows. At times, a homeless Shravak or Shravika, or one aspiring to become a monk or nun in the near future can actually live in the Upashraya. The Sangha soon finds an appropriate occupation and a place to live, for the destitute ones.

An Upashraya is a holy residence, and its dignity and its atmosphere should be maintained. It is also a place where many religious functions are held. It is not a place for a picnic, party, socialization, or entertainment. In America, instead of Upashrayas we use school auditoriums, gyms, or other halls. The same code of behavior applies there, when that place is used as an Upashraya.

Food is permitted in an Upashraya. Some cooking is also permitted. The food and its processing and cooking should be according to Jain principles, e.g. no meat, eggs, fish etc., no potatoes, onions, or carrots either. In addition, there are many other restrictions.

Often, especially in America, the religious functions are marred by children running around, Shravaks and Shravikas talking loudly and socializing, or feeding babies meat and other unacceptable baby food, etc. All it takes is a little thinking to realize that in a way, all these acts are violence against the Jinas and their Sangha.

An Upashraya is sacred because that is where the monks and nuns who are on the path to self-realization, live, practice and preach. Also Shravaks and Shravikas go there to practice the same religion, and aspire to be (but not necessarily so) monks and nuns. Let us now look at these monks and nuns who are one step ahead of us.

8. MONKS AND NUNS

These are the flag bearers of the Jinas. They study, and spread the word of the Jinas. They practice it all day and all night. They have given up everything else in pursuit of the truth as the Jinas outlined. They have chosen very high standards and the hard life that goes with that.

They were once Shravaks and Shravikas, but they gave up their civilian life – their parents, spouse, children, house, business, possessions, everything – to follow the path of the Jinas. They live with their Guru and his other disciples.

They do not keep, take or give any money, either directly or indirectly. They keep only a few sets of clothes and the wooden containers to bring food to the Upashraya. They do not shop or cook. They go from door to door, unannounced and take a small amount of acceptable food from Jain and other homes. They do not accept anything that is cooked just for them. They do not take anything that is still on the stove.

They do not ask for any special food items. When they do accept food, it all goes in one container, and it mixes with other food. They eat everything they accept. They do not save, preserve, or discard anything. They do not re-warm or season the food.

This practice of gathering food, by going from house to house, and taking only a little from each place, is called **'Gochari'**. This is a very interesting word, and it means, 'as a cow grazes'. Not many of us may know, that unlike sheep and other animals, a cow does not eat up all the grass and leave a bare ground behind. 'Go' or 'Gau' (as in Gautama, the Buddha) means 'a cow', and 'Chara' means 'to walk' or 'to graze'.

These monks, Sadhus and Sadhvis, do not use any appliances, electricity or vehicles. They do not use microphones. They go barefoot from place to place. Even the religious books, the monks can keep very few. They do not touch a member of the opposite sex ever. They are always in Samayika, every minute of their life. Therefore, they can get up and go to bathroom, etc. during a Pratikramana. Shravaks and Shravikas preferably should not.

They do not get haircuts. They pull their own hairs off periodically. Yes, it hurts, and it bleeds. This act is called **Lunchana**. Sadhus of the

70

Digambara (Dig = directions - east, west, etc. - i.e. sky, Ambara (rhymes with 'plumber') = clothing. Literally, 'sky-clad') sect do not wear any clothing. They generally live in forests. There are no Digambara nuns like that. Apparently, an exposed male body cannot hide any disturbed emotions. On the other hand, an exposed female body actually can stir up emotions. This sect does not believe that women can achieve salvation. However, it still does not otherwise treat them as inferior.

Shvetambara (Shveta = white) monks wear white or yellow clothes. They live in the Upashraya. They walk from one town to other, barefoot, carrying their meager possessions. During the four months of rainy season, called *Chaumasun* (Chau = four, Masa = months), they do not travel, but stay in one Upashraya. Monks do not wade through water unnecessarily, nor do they go out in the rain. They always use boiled water for everything.

Monks do Tapas, they study, write books and prayers, etc. They preach also. When they go from door to door, and from town to town, they meet Shravaks and Shravikas, and discuss religion with them, and guide them in their conduct. They speak to children and teach them. They generally stay out of personal matters but may help patch up differences and disputes. They preach scriptures and guide religious observances. They advise building new temples, Upashrayas, libraries, and preserving the old ones.

They practice extreme non-violence, truth, celibacy, and they keep no possessions. They do not brush their teeth. There are some changes visible now. There are a few monks who have come to the United States by air-plane, and they do travel by car. They and some others use microphones also. Some of these of course brush their teeth. They eat the food cooked for them. There are only a handful of such monks, and their practices have stirred up controversy in India.

We can only be thankful to them, our Gurus, for the benefits we can get from their presence. We don't have to be judgmental about this in absence of an alternative. However, it should be pointed out that even though the Sadhus and the Sadhvis are one step ahead of the Shravaks and Shravikas, and even though Sadhus are the Gurus, it is the Sangha that is the final authority, and the Sangha can command monks and nuns. This power is exercised on extremely rare occasions, but it has been, indeed. Such are the checks and balances in the **Shasana** (reign) of our Jinas.

Now we know what the Sangha and its four components, the Sadhu, Sadhvi, Shravak and Shravika do and don't do. We visited the house-hold, and the Upashraya where Jina's teachings are practised. We looked at the fundamental principles on which these practices are based. We also talked about controlling our mind and our body, with and without the help of a few rituals. All these rituals were directed at us, and at our Gurus who are actually our fellow travellers on the path shown by the Jinas.

Now we are ready to meet the Jinas, and to sit down at their feet. We are ready to thank them and praise them for the endless and boundless mercy they have shown upon us. Let us leave all the discussions, rituals, and other things behind, and go to the Jina's temple.

10. THE TEMPLE

The Jain temple is also known as a Jinalaya, Jina Mandira, Derasara, etc. It is the holy place where the Jina's idol (statue) presides over the Sangha. It is said that the temples are Jainism's unique contribution to the Indian culture. There were no real temples before Jainism.

A temple is a very clean, holy place where we go to worship the idol. There is no food, cooking or lectures in the temple. None of the rituals we talked about, are practiced there. Ideally, one does not talk to anybody else about anything in the temple. All talk is with the Lord.

Jain temples are very ornate and decorative. Many are the finest examples of architecture and sculpture. They can be in a town or a city, but many well-known ones are on the tops of mountains. Some are more than a thousand years old. The temples are made from marble, and they have many glass chandeliers with oil lamps within. These create a very pleasant, quiet and spiritual atmosphere. Now electric light bulbs have changed that in almost all temples.

There is a big hall in which the members of the Sangha sit or stand during the worship. This hall is well decorated as described earlier. At the end of the hall, usually behind a door, is a much smaller inner sanctum, called the **Garbha Dvara** (Garbha = a fetus, inner; Dvara = a door) in which the Lord's idol is placed.

The Garbha Dvara is absolutely without any decoration, sculpture, or the like. It does not need all that. It is very plain, simple and austere. It has its own light, the light of all lights, the Lord. The Sangha needs light, art and all the other things.

Derasara or Jinalaya (Alaya = abode, a place. Remember the Himalayas? Hima = ice or snow) is a very special place. Whatever you are not supposed to do in the house or in an Upashraya, you cannot do in the temple either, and there is much more.

You should go to the temple preferably in the morning, just after taking a bath, before you start your day. You can go there at any time of the day from about 6 am to about 9 pm. You can say prayers, take part in ceremonies or in temple rituals, make an offering of money, fruits, sweets, and so on.

One cannot take anything from a Jain temple. The fruits and sweets, etc. offered to the Lord are distributed among the poor. One should not take any fruits and other items to the temple either, except as an offering. If you take it there, you should leave it there.

Eating anything, including candy or a chewing gum is forbidden in a Jain temple. Actually, one is supposed to rinse one's mouth before going there. Hindu temples, on the other hand have a tradition of offering food to the Lord and then distributing it among the devotees as a blessing (**Prasada**) from the Lord.

In the United States, there are many multi-denominational temples (i.e., with idols from different religions) in which Lord Mahavira and other Tirthankaras take their thrones side by side with Lord Krishna, Shiva, etc. This is laudatory, and one should not create divisions, but a Jain should refrain from eating in the temple.

One can enter the inner sanctum or Garbha Dvara, only after taking a bath, and putting on very clean clothes to physically touch and worship the idol with flowers, saffron and other objects. Utmost care and respect are called for. This **Puja** (worship) can be easily learned properly from someone who knows.

Even without entering the **Gabharo**, as the Garbha Dvara is commonly called, there are many other ways to do the worship. One can say prayers, shine a lamp, present incense, etc. One or more members of the Sangha can sit down in the temple hall, with or without simple musical instruments and sing elaborate Pujas of various kinds, lasting for just a few minutes to as long as a week, not counting the nights.

In the evening, there are rituals of **Arati** ('pleading') and of **Mangala Divo** (Holy Lamp) in each of which, lamps are lighted in a plate, and prayers are said. Then the temple closes for the night. No one can live in the temple.

Not all Jains worship the idol. Those who do are called **Murti-Pujaka** (idol worshipper). Of these, some decorate the idol, others do not. Some do not even have temples. They have something like an Upashraya only, called a **Sthanaka** ('a place' of the Lord). They are all Jains, and they all believe in the same fundamental principles. To understand these various practices, let us first understand what the purpose of a temple is, and what is behind the **Murti Puja.**

11. MURTI PUJA

Almost all Hindus, most Buddhists, and a majority of Jains worship idols. But, according to many thinkers and sages in India and outside, Murti Puja or idol worship is nonsense. Jewish and Christian faiths forbid it, Islam is against it. Zoroastrians do not believe in it. Many Jains do not believe in it either.

We are not here to pass judgement on who is right and who is not. Although, I am a Murti Pujaka Jain, I do not feel compelled to defend it either. It is a personal matter between my Lord and myself, and Lord Mahavira has preached tolerance based on the principle of the Multiplicity of Viewpoints.

Everybody is right, to an extent at least. On the other hand, when we are all lost, it is futile to argue over who is lost more, and who is farther from the truth. We can only decide that after we find the truth, and that's what we are trying to do - find the truth. To find the truth is to find our salvation and freedom, and ourselves. It is all one and the same.

We carry pictures of our loved ones in our pockets. We create statues of our national and other heroes. The Zoroastrians worship the fire, the Christians respect the cross and kneel in front of it. Almost all of us salute the flag of our nation, 'and the republic for which it stands, one nation under God, indivisible, with Liberty, and Justice for all'.

Everybody knows that the piece of paper on which the photograph is printed, is not really our grandma, and the piece of cloth, which we call a flag, is not really our nation. We all can agree that the idol is not the Lord, although there is a Hindu sect which actually treats the idols as God. They are free to believe what they want. All religions call God to be omnipresent, that is, present everywhere, in everything. So it will be difficult to say that God is not present in stone idols!

Our beloved nation certainly does not reside in the flag. No arguments about that. Still we accord the flag a position of great honor, in all our ceremonies, and in the battles against our external enemies, and are willing to even die for it. All this, even though the flag in no way resembles our country, nor does it carry a map of our country on it.

The flag stands for our republic. The idol stands for our Lord. We accept on faith, a dollar bill which is only a sheet of worthless paper, because the full force of the Federal Government is behind it. Similarly, we accept the idol to represent the Lord, because the full faith of the Jain Sangha stands behind it. We know that the Lord is there, because we put Him there.

He is there only *if* we put him there. In worshipping the idol, we worship our faith. If we have no faith, we cannot worship the Lord, be it in stone, a piece of paper, a piece of cloth, or whatever. As it is, it is difficult to have faith in a God that we cannot see or feel. Putting Him in stone does not make it any easier. Then, why complicate the matter?

For a very good reason. The temple is like a post office. We go there to send our prayers addressed to the Lord. If the Lord is sitting there, we can address Him directly. We can send letters to Santa Claus also, if we believe he is there at the North Pole. The real question is not whether the Lord is present in the stone, or in anything else. We couldn't care less, and many of us really don't.

The real issue is whether the Lord is present in our hearts, in our minds, and in our soul. We go to the temple post office to send a message to the Lord, for Him or Her to come and stay with us, or at least visit us. Once (S)He comes in our body, and is present in everything we do, our body and our selves become a temple. Then of course we see Him in every grain of sand, and in anything and everything around us. That's the purpose of Murti Puja. If you can achieve that otherwise, and we do know that it can be done, that's fine too.

There are several ways of worshipping the Lord. We can do it by chanting His name, or by worshipping His idol or picture. We can do these with some objects or only with our feelings. The best is of course with our feelings of devotion. Chanting helps reinforce that. We can offer various objects to the idol with the same purpose. There are several objects and substances including water, light, fragrant sandalwood, flowers, etc. which can be offered.

All these are only symbolic. Bathing the idol, making it shine in the light, or making it fragrant, are not really meant for the idol at all. They are meant for us. We purify ourselves, and make our lives fragrant and shining. That's the wish, that's the prayer. We are actually washing and purifying our soul, which is basically no different from that of the Jinas.

12. BUT WHY DO WE WORSHIP THE JINAS ?

We should address this question which has plagued the minds of many Jains. None of our Tirthankaras is God. They do not take birth as incarnations to help us out. They do not appear when we pray to them, and help us out with our Math exam or with our Calculus quiz. They do not perform any miracles.

Still worse, they don't even order us to do something that will please them. When we don't follow the path shown by them, they do not get mad, and even if they do, they do not show their wrath on us. So the question is, why in the world should we worship the Jinas and the Tirthankaras?

A very good question. Let me try to answer it. We live in a very selfish world, where we don't just give something for nothing, even to the Jinas. They taught us that we should not be afraid of any one, even God. We should not wait for someone to come and get us out of trouble. Actually, they showed us how we can do that ourselves.

We do not have to worship an external power that is awe-inspiring, or can get mad with us. They put the key in our hands. With that we can set ourselves free. True, they do not get pleased or displeased with us. But they really felt compassion for us. They saw that we are ignorant and are suffering. We are trapped, and we don't even know that we have the key to open all locks and set us free. They showed us the way. But we keep on forgetting it. By worshipping them, we remind ourselves of what they said, and are being thankful to them.

They do not want us to worship them. They do not want anything from us. They want us to be free, independent, knowledgeable and fearless, so that we won't start worshipping anything or anybody out of greed or fear, or out of our selfish dependence, or out of petty desires.

The Jinas showed us that if this world is an illusion, then God is the biggest illusion of all. Once you get true knowledge the illusion disappears, and you see everything, including God, for what it really is. Then, armed with the proper knowledge and the proper vision, with our proper actions, we are as capable as anybody else. We won't need a God then.

God works through us. 'We are That', as the Hindu scriptures say. We have worshipped various God(s) and gods and our bodies and our minds for a very long time, which was a waste. So we are thankful to the Jinas for showing us the right path, and that we are no different from them. But why in the world do we worship the Jinas? The answer is simple. Because we want to!

Now we know the Sangha, its institutions, its rituals, and we also know the principles and practices of the Jain Shasana (realm, reign). Let us now have a big celebration to invite and meet the Tirthankaras. For that, the whole Sangha has to come together, and settle down.

13. FESTIVALS

THE PARYUSHANA PARVA

Parva means a festival. Paryushana is the name of it. In the monsoon, or the rainy season (June - September) in India, travelling becomes difficult, and the whole countryside comes to life with all kinds of insects, worms, moss, and what not. The rains flood the rivers and the lakes, washing all types of stuff in them, including the eggs and spores of harmful disease spreading agents. The rain is good for the crops and is of course essential, but if it rains for days and days, it can get depressing. That is the best time to get the Sangha together to do some worthwhile things.

Paryushana means 'settling down'. Shravaks and Shravikas cannot travel much because of the rains. Sadhus and Sadhvis are not permitted to travel during the monsoon. The skies are dark, mood is gloomy, and conditions are unhealthy. What other time could be better to think about the Jinas, and the lamps they have lighted for us?

Why not do the Tapas that foster good health? Why not patch up differences and make up with one another? Why not look at the temples after the rains to see and repair the damage? Why not read the religious books lest they get soggy and moldy? With all the floods swelling around us, why not read and hear the life of Lord Mahavira and his apostles (first disciples, called **Ganadharas**. Gana = group, Dhara = to hold up), who prepared the dock (Tirtha) for us to take the boat across?

Paryushana Parva lasts for eight days, including the last four days of the tenth month Shravana and the first four days of the eleventh month Bhadrapada. The months are named after the constellations of the stars. During these days we go to the Derasara, and to the Upashraya, to listen to the the Acharya deliver the Vyakhyana. We do various fasts, partial or complete, one or more. The last one is always on the last day of the Paryushana Parva, called Samvatsari.

Samvatsari is the day of the biggest Pratikramana to review all possible sins and to apologize for them. It is also for forgiving one another and to become friends again. You can understand after what we have discussed so far, that when we forgive someone we are doing a favor to ourselves, not to them. So no matter how strongly other people feel against us, it is not relevant. We must forgive them. They may hate us, but we just don't. We are free.

What better way to destroy
an enemy than to make
him/her a friend?

During Paryushana, the Acharya reads and explains the the the holy Kalpa Sutra to the Sangha. The Kalpa Sutra describes the life of Lord Mahavira, and the early days of the Sangha. The Kalpa Sutra has 1200 stanzas, therefore it is called Barasa (1200) Sutra, or a 'necklace of twelve hundred beads.'

On the fifth day of Paryushana, he reads sections from the Kalpa Sutra, regarding the birth of our beloved Lord Mahavira, the great victor. The whole Sangha listens and rejoices.

When the Lord was conceived, his mother had seen fourteen dreams. The images of these dreams are shown to the Sangha which greets and worships these dreams. This ceremony runs for several hours, and the Sangha awaits the birth of the Lord. No other reading is done during the ceremony, except the one line stating that the Lord is born.

The whole ritual consists of many Vidhis and it generates significant and much needed income for the Derasara. However, it can hardly be called interesting, or educational or conducive to religious feelings. In some places severe discipline problems stem up, and within the limits of the Jina's words, some improvements would be welcome. For our part, we should know about the dreams and their importance, and teach the children about them, to put some meaning into this wonderful event.

Lord Mahavira was not born on this day. We read about his birth on this day. The dreams foretold what the child was going to be like. One should hear this from the Acharya, during Paryushana, but we can look at them briefly.

THE FOURTEEN DREAMS

A dream is called 'Swapna' in Sanskrit, so we talk about the fourteen Sapanas or Supanas. The Lord's mother saw these bright and shining. They are holy and pure. They indicate knowledge, wealth, strength, and other good qualities.

(i)	An elephant.	Loyalty, strength, wisdom.
(ii)	An ox.	Strength.
(iii)	A lion.	The king of the forest.
(iv)	Goddess Laxmi.	Wealth.
(v)	A flower garland.	Fragrant life.
(vi)	The Moon.	Cool light.
(vii)	The Sun.	Brightness, warmth.
(viii)	Orange flag.	Sacrifice, renunciation
(ix)	Full water-pot.	A rich, deep, meaningful life.
(x)	Lotus lake.	Tranquility and detachment.
(xi)	An ocean.	Full of depth and gems.
(xii)	An airplane.	Lofty height of the soul.
(xiii)	A pile of gems.	Worthiness, luster.
(xiv)	A smokeless flame.	Pure knowledge.

These dreams are symbolic of good qualities that the Lord stands for. There seems to be an order in this apparently disorderly listing of dreams. The most important is the last one. That is Kevala Gnyana, the highest level an Atma can reach. On the other hand, the first and the second dreams – those of an elephant, and a bull – signify untamed energy. That is the state of an Atma which is still full of ignorance.

It is likely that these dreams suggest the steps of enlightenment of an Atma. Interestingly, there are fourteen such steps described, known as **Guna-sthanakas** ('virtue stations'). This is a reminder for the assembled Sangha to give up apathy, and to resume climbing the ladder of virtue, that is to go from the Atma to become a Paramatma.

These are our dreams, or they should be. For someone in bondage, what could be a more cherished dream than freedom or the Kevala Gnyana and the Moksha?

CHAITYA PARIPATI

Chaitya means, a chapel, or a temple. *Paripati* means "to wander" (Compare the English word *Peripatetic*, meaning, a wanderer). Chaitya Paripati means visiting all the nearby temples, within an appropriate range. At the end of the Paryushana, the Sangha should visit all the temples. It is good to move about a little, meet the members of other Sanghas and help them build or restore the temples. All this should be done well before we get back into our day to day business, and forget what we always meant to do.

The biggest Atichara is
failing to do
what we could have easily done.

DIWALI

Diwali is the festival of lights. Diwali is to India as what Christmas is to the Christian world. The word Diwali comes from Deep (a lamp), and Awali (a series, a chain). It is the last day of the Hindu year (1992 A.D. is the 2049th year of the king Vikrama). It is celebrated as a cultural festival by many people in India. In general, it indicates the end of the darkness and a time for light, the end of evil, and victory of good.

For Jains, it indicates a different kind of light. That is the day Lord Mahavira's soul reached its freedom from the body (that is, he died), leaving the eternal flame of knowledge for us. It is a solemn occasion, but it does not prevent one from joining the festive celebrations of Diwali.

MAHAVIRA JAYANTI

This is the real birthday of the Lord. It falls on the 13th day of the month Chaitra, the 6th month of the Hindu calendar, (around April in the Christian calendar. The Hindu New Year comes in October or November). It is celebrated with lectures, seminars and conferences on the Lord's teachings on non-violence, world peace, and the environmental issues. The Sapana watching and the celebration of the Lord's birth on the 5th day of Paryushana has nothing to do with the Lord's birthday. On that day the Sangha reads about the birth of Lord Mahavira from the Kalpa Sutra.

15.   JAINISM AND HEALTH

It may seem as if all the Vratas, Tapas, and rituals are devised to torture our body and kill our mind, because the Atma is the only thing that matters! Nothing could be further from the truth. Let me explain.

Suppose you want to go to meet an important person. So you hire a taxicab. It can happen that the cab is not in the perfect mechanical condition, nor is it clean or comfortable. The driver is impolite, and nasty with you and with other drivers and he drives unsafely. To make it worse, he doesn't even know his way around the town.

You can easily guess that the cab is our body, and the driver is our mind. We are, of course, the Atma. To continue our example, we cannot just get off the taxicab, and start walking. We need both, the cab and its driver too.

We have to instruct the driver to be polite, to stop smoking, to turn the radio off, and to get his cab's flat tire fixed. We want to have the driver and the cab in good order to complete our journey safely.

A healthy body and a healthy mind are essential for our spiritual pursuit; but we cannot afford to pamper them so much so that we forget what they are meant for. They have to be in good condition. They should respond well to our commands.

Good physical and mental health are very useful in acquiring spiritual health, although a weak person can also be spiritually strong. Our pursuit of spiritual health is not at the expense of our physical and mental well being. Actually, we develop a good body and a good mind on our way in any case.

Although I am a physician, I am not giving any medical advice here. As a matter of fact, medicine knows far more about disease and its treatment than what it knows about health. Some diseases (car accidents, stab wounds, etc.) can overpower even the healthiest body and mind. But generally, it is the lack of health that invites disease.

Just as the body and the mind are only the tools to do something, health is also a tool. It is not an end in itself. We want to be at mental peace, and in good physical health to find our true self. Religious practice can make you healthy, but that is not its goal or purpose, it is only a fringe benefit.

From what you have read so far, you can easily see for yourself that many of the items covered under good conduct (Achara) and the Vratas are healthy practices. Not eating during the dark hours before sunrise or after sunset is prudent, as is drinking only boiled water.

Not keeping the food overnight as leftovers can prevent many cases of food-poisoning. A Vegetarian diet can keep your cholesterol low, since vegetable oils contain no cholesterol. They contain fat nonetheless. Dairy products, including Ghee (clarified butter) are high in cholesterol.

Not killing animals, and not swatting the flies, mosquitoes and other insects can prevent your contact with their disease-carrying body fluids.

Partial or total fasting, if done judiciously cannot hurt. It can save food for yourself and for others. From the point of view of dieting to lose weight, its value is limited, but the self control you gain is priceless. Self control, by itself can prevent weight gain.

Controlling one's sex drive is wise, and not lusting after someone else's girlfriend or wife is safe. Channeling the creative power of the sex drive into the arts, sports, etc. can make one healthy and successful. However, the relationship between celibacy and health is an indirect one.

Not all religious practices can be called healthy though. Not brushing your teeth during a fast, for example. We are not saying anything for or against that. One can argue whether or not such practices are unhealthy, but no one considers them to be healthy. The purpose of the ritual is spiritual health, rather than physical.

Fasting may be dangerous for someone who is suffering from Diabetes, but not necessarily so. Common sense should prevail in such matters, and medical advice may be necessary. Dying during a ritual neither helps the person who dies, nor does it further the cause of the religion.

There is nothing healthy about fasting as a spectator sport, or about any Tapa done to keep up with the Joneses. Religion does not primarily try to make you healthy, and it should not make you sick either. Once again, you are the boss, and you are responsible for your health.

16. WOMEN SEX AND ABORTIONS

In a famous story (of king Akbara and his witty friend and courtier Birbal), there is a rapidly filling pool of water, in which a monkey tries to keep her baby afloat by lifting it. Finally, when the water gets too high, she pushes the baby underwater, and stands upon it to save herself. Even societies, when subjected to conditions of deprivation and desperation, reach for such solutions.

Almost all societies have, at one time or another, allowed one of their subgroups to come up at the expense of another. One race, class, or sex may be better placed to achieve a goal, and menbers of that group may be encouraged with greater optimism to achieve it. This should not mean that the trailing group has no hope. In the long run, all running races are, after all between rabbits and tortoises. With enough determination and perseverance, anybody can succeed.

WOMEN

One question invariably comes up: 'Can women achieve salvation?' Let me answer that promptly, before we discuss further. The answer is, YES ! Women can achieve salvation, and can help men in doing so as well.

Women can achieve salvation,
and they can
help men in doing so as well.

The question of salvation for women, although important in principle, is of hardly any practical significance. For even men are not achieving their salvation nowadays. In a strange way, we have achieved equality!

The condition of women in India today leaves much to be desired. Without trying to defend or condone that, one can say that the women's condition is determined by biological, cultural, historical and socioeconomic factors. Indian religions in general, and Jainism in particular give women equal status.

At least one of the Tirthankaras (Malli Natha, the 19th Tirthankara) was a woman. We will see her story in the Part III. Lord Mahavira's and the other Tirthankaras' mothers and wives are also highly respected. The Jain archives are full of stories of illustrious Shravikas and Sadhvis.

However, Jainism flourished in a male-dominated society. Therefore, at least culturally, women do defer to men. Most Acharyas are men. So almost all preachers are men. Sadhvis do not preach, or lead the rituals of Pratikramana when a male Acharya is around. This is not always the case and Sadhvis do preach and lead the Sangha in rituals. I have seen Shravikas standing up to powerful Acharyas when a disagreement occurs.

Menstruating women are advised not to go into the temple nor engage in idol worship. This is because of the perceived uncleanliness, and even men are advised to observe this if they have any wound or an ulcer that is bleeding or oozing pus.

In the morning Pratikramana, Jains remember great Jain civilians and monks in a prayer which begins with 'Bharahesara Bahubali...'. It lists almost an equal number of men and women. There is at least one story that goes with each name. You may ask your parents and teachers about this. Many women have achieved Moksha, and by their illustrious examples, have led many other men and women on their path to salvation. Women are not considered 'bad'. Shravikas have same rights as Shravaks.

MARRIAGE AND SEX

Lord Mahavira and other Tirthankaras were born in the same way as everybody else is born. Jainism does not talk about the 'Virgin Mother' or the 'Immaculate (clean, stain-less) conception' unlike Christianity. Sex is not taboo, nor is it banned, nor is it considered bad. It is part of life. There are sexual carvings in a few Hindu and Jain temples also (e.g. Khajuraho). Such carvings remind us to leave all such worldly attractions and temptations outside, and then enter the temple.

Jainism emphasizes the transient nature of our bodies, and advocates a detached attitude towards it. If our own body is not ours, how can someone else's body be ours? Once one learns to control one's self, and progresses on the path to liberating one's Atma, sex naturally takes a secondary place.

Marital sex is recognized and accepted. Extramarital or premarital sex is not, of course. Even marital sex is something one is supposed to rise above and eventually give up. Our bodies and our energy have many other and better uses. Once Shravaks and Shravikas learn to control their sex drive, they can become Sadhus and Sadhvis. Monks are not permitted to engage in any kind of sexual activities.

BIRTH CONTROL AND ABORTIONS

Understandably, Jainism does not comment directly on contraceptives or birth-control devices. Its emphasis is on self control. Failing that, anything you can do to protect yourself and your partner is up to you. Contraceptives may prevent pregnancy, or some diseases, but one should remember that uncontrolled sexual activity is the biggest disease, and can get one into deep trouble. I have not found anything in Jainism that prohibits the use of contraceptives by a legally married couple.

Jainism treats us as mature and responsible persons. It explains everything, and teaches how to judge right from wrong. It leaves the practice up to us, and recognizes our limitations. It appreciates the power of the monkey mind, and that of the sex drive. But it also knows that we are capable of overcoming that and of taking charge to become our own masters. It is waiting patiently for us to find our selves.

ALCOHOL AND OTHER DRUGS

Taking alcohol to relax, and taking drugs to stimulate our mind and body, or increasing our sex drive (actually, alcohol and other drugs decrease it, and impair one's performance) can only make us forget ourselves, and can take us in the wrong direction. If you take these substances, you are working against yourself.

If one behaves responsibly, avoids taking drugs including alcohol, avoids engaging in extramarital and premarital sex, and plans one's family with proper control practices, then the question of abortion should not come up. Lawyers can debate when life begins, and when abortion becomes murder. For a religion which advocates against eating even non-fertile eggs, any abortion is murder.

But you are the judge. If you're careful, you won't need an abortion. Even if you have been careful and now you need an abortion, wake up! Make up your mind to take control of your life. Talk to your partner, parents, teachers, friends, anyone. Go to a physician. Don't die of guilt and shame.

Even if you cannot meet the more stringent religious standards, at least observe the law of the land. But next time, be careful. Jainism will not throw you into prison or into hell. But you could end up in either of these places, if you are not careful. Return to the Jinas as soon as you can!

17. CONTRIBUTIONS OF JAINISM

Over the 2500 plus years that Jainism as preached by Lord Mahavira has existed, Jains have made very many significant contributions, and have played a significant role in the history of the human race.

Jains have made outstanding contributions in the fields of literature, art, architecture, and sculpture. Their contribution by way of the principles of non-violence, multiplicity of viewpoints, and of preserving the environment are quite noteworthy. They have produced a huge body of philosophical literature. They have produced innumerable manuscripts, temples, and educational and charitable institutions for people and for animals. Jainism has produced many outstanding people. Now let us turn to some of their contributions.

All religions try to change or control human nature, and try to teach its followers to live in harmony and at peace with themselves and with the rest of the universe. They all try to destroy evil, and bring out the good. They are all unique in some way or other. Over the long history, and during pre-historic periods, there have been many prophets who have started various faiths.

Whether these prophets are considered to be God, incarnations of God, demi-gods, or enlightened souls, they all did the same thing. Because they were born in different cultural and geographical conditions at different times, their ways of presenting the Truth had to be different. At times, the monkey minds of their followers, especially the blind followers, could not see the basic similarities in their teachings.

As a result, the very idea of religion, which was to foster harmony, led to a great deal of disharmony instead. 'Faith' itself became a bad word for the so-called thinking, learned and educated people. But they were no less confused themselves. They failed to see the good in all this, and discarded or avoided religion altogether. Harmony among religions is at least as important as it is among various people.

Jainism's greatest contribution is **tolerance.** Its principles of Non-Violence and of the **Multiplicity of Viewpoints** are at the root of this. Tolerance is a limited term. Jainism's tolerance implies no reluctance. It is acceptance, brotherhood, equality, and love.

Its tolerance extends to, and permeates every little corner of life. It does not believe in the caste system. There are no untouchables. It gives **equal rights to women.** It gives authority to the Sangha, even over the monks.

Its principle of **Non-Violence** was turned into a tremendous moral and political force by Mahatma Gandhi, who was not born a Jain. Recently, within the past 3-4 years (1987-1991), the political changes that took place without violence, in Germany, Eastern Europe, and the Soviet Union, including the overthrowing, changing or restoring of governments, plus the change that was attempted in the mainland China, and the struggle of the African Americans for equal rights, can all be traced back to Gandhiji and to Jainism.

The **environmental concerns** arising out of the destruction of the habitat, production of waste, and severe pollution, can be attributed in part to profit-making and hoarding by the industrial establishment. The principles of non-hoarding and of making do with the least possible, advocated by Jainism, are an answer to that. Protecting wildlife, including every blade of grass and every earthworm is the way out.

Vegetarianism is part of Hinduism and Buddhism also, but it is most emphasized by Jainism. Today vegetarianism is most prevalent in the State of Gujarat where Jainism has its stronest following.

Jainism's very important contribution is to **make the individual responsible** for his or her own actions, by removing the ideas of God as the judge, and of destiny. One does not have to be afraid of anyone, not even God. One does not have to please anybody, not even God.

Punyas do not cancel out Papas. You rejoice or suffer for both in sequence. Neither you, nor anyone else can 'wash' your sins away. **God is a figurehead** in this democracy. You are the prime minister. God acts depending upon your reports and 'advice'.

Jainism did another thing by making the individual responsible. It prevented the individual from blaming everybody else. If something needs to be done, you do it if you can, and as much as you can. You cannot blame others.

The idea of self-control, rather than authority or power over others, prevents an individual from making big beginnings and setting up very large projects just to make personal profit. It also helps keep one from squandering away precious resources under the name of some narrow definition of progress.

Towards this end, Jainism introduced the ideas of **Upayoga** ('control', to use judiciously) and of **Jayana** ('nurturing', not destroying it). When one does anything, i.e., talk, stretch oneself, or use water, one should keep 'Upayoga', that is talk slowly so as not to disturb anyone else, stretch in a way so as not to punch someone's nose, and use water without wasting. These are not really negative in tone. Use it, just don't abuse it.

When you see something, don't use it inadvertently as a weapon. Use Jayana or care. When you walk, don't step on an animal, don't pour boiling water into anything without looking, don't put firewood in the fire without shaking off any creatures that it may harbor. This is not ridiculous. Even if you don't care a bit for them, it is for your own good too.

You don't want to step on a snake, pour boiling water into the kitchen sink while your husband is working underneath, or be bitten by a scorpion hiding in the firewood. Everything you do, do it with 'Upayoga' and with utmost 'Jayana'. If not, you will either run out of it, or will get only ruined by it.

Upayoga and Jayana are observed while dealing with objects, while **Jivadaya** is observed in dealing with animals. (Jiva = life, Daya = mercy, pity). It means having compassion for all the living beings. When dealing with pets, beasts of burden, circus animals, or those which give us milk, treat them with kindness.

When a cow stops giving milk, it doesn't automatically have to go to a slaughterhouse. Yes, even if that means loss of some profit. If it served you all its life, you must serve it till its life ends.

But higher than everything else, including non-violence and Jivadaya, is **Knowledge.** Jainism's highest emphasis is on knowledge. The true knowledge, when combined with the understanding and right action (The Three Gems) leads us to salvation. Out of this great respect for knowledge, Jains have built countless libraries and schools.

Every temple and Upashraya contains many ancient manuscripts. Books are favorite gifts on religious occasions. The fifth day of the Hindu year is called Gnyana Panchami (Gnyana = knowledge, Panchami = the fifth of the month, here the fifth of the first month), when knowledge is worshipped.

Jains are great **temple builders.** The temples as we know today are a gift of Jainism. Before that, Hindus made their offerings to fire, or did their purification in a river. There are temple cities such as Palitana, Giranara, Samet Shikhara and Mount Abu which are famous holy places of pilgrimage. Mount Abu is the home of Delwada temples famous for their wax-like marble carvings. You have to see these, to believe how lovely they are.

Jainism has had tremendous **influence on literature.** Jain literature itself is vast, and most of it is in Sanskrit and in Ardha-Magadhi. The later day writings are in Gujarati and Hindi. Actually, Jain monks are the ones who started writing the early versions of what we now call the **Gujarati language.** A well-known Jain Acharya Hemchandracharya wrote the first **Gujarati grammar.** Actually, it was the grammar of a parent language of old Gujarati language. Jain monks wrote a number of prayers and other religious poems.

Jainism took great strides in **astrology,** and in the **Occult** also. Its influence on the science is also noteworthy. Apart from environmental concerns, and non-violence, the idea of **plants as living beings** is rooted in Jainism. The idea of relativity in Physics is predated by the relativity of the Truth, in Jainism.

18. JAINISM
WITH WARTS AND ALL

Like other religions, Jainism puts an ideal in front of us in the form of the Siddhas, who are the perfect beings. We can elevate ourselves and potentially become Siddhas. But we are not perfect, not yet anyway.

In these pages I have drawn a somewhat idealized picture of Jainism and of Jains. In real life, people are people, and we are not different than anybody else. Jainism may be the best way to salvation, but nothing is perfect. It has been criticized rightly and wrongly on several aspects.

Non-violence, the very basis of Jainism, is also a cause for criticism. Based on this good principle, Jain youths stay away from the police force, the military and from agriculture. There may be many reasons for this behavior, religion being only one of them.

Jainism's stronghold is in the state of Gujurata, and especially among the well-to-do business people. They are adventurous, and have entrepreneurship in business ventures. Since these Jains are well-to-do, they may be less inclined, and still less compelled, to go into the military and/or agricultural occupations. Their religion may have nothing to do with this.

Jainism does not forbid anything. It does advocate non-violence to the extent it is practical. The police force, the military, fire-fighting, and farming are essential and important professions. The medical profession is another one.

I was born and brought up in a Jain family, right in the middle of one of the biggest centers of Jainism. When I joined a medical school, no one around me was upset. Yes, I do prefer to avoid animal experiments, and medicines of animal origins, but I accept both in the interest of my patients, pending any alternatives.

We should remember that when someone else does farming or fire fighting for us, it does not relieve us of our responsibility. Therefore, whether we do (Karana) the agriculture or not, is not the issue. As long as it is done on our behalf (Karavana, and Anumodana), it is done by us. We might as well do it ourselves. That's the way I see it. The conservatives may disagree. You may want to discuss this point with your teacher.

Some of us are money lenders, and some among us are loan sharks. It is said that these Jains will filter water before drinking, but will drink blood just like that! This is not the fault of Jainism which actually gets a bad name from bad Jains. Hypocrisy is bad at all times.

The other issue is that of health. Jains claim that a vegetarian diet, not eating before sunrise and after sunset, and drinking boiled water are conducive to good health. This is understandable. On the other hand, not brushing teeth during fasting by the civilians, and not brushing the teeth ever by the monks have generated derogatory remarks from others, as well as some dissenting voices from among Jains. Rinsing the mouth with boiled water is possible, and on the other hand, poor hygiene can co-exist with daily brushing also. Common sense and some flexibility can certainly go a long way.

The next item is not a criticism, but rather a drawback. Jain Sadhus and Sadhvis do not use any electrical appliances or motor vehicles. They do not use microphones, cars, trains or air planes. This makes it very difficult for Jains living abroad to see their monks, and very difficult for those in India to hear their sermons and the Jinas' message.

Those monks who have come to the U.S.A. use microphones, motor cars, and air planes. Some even record their sermons on audio and video tapes. The Sangha will have to decide in the best interest of the Sangha and of the Shasana (reign) of the Jinas.

Jainism is said to be very strict. It is rather stern, and its practice involves lot of fasting, walking barefoot, and according to some, torturing the body. Its non-violence is extreme, as are its rituals of apologizing for all the wrong doings. Apparently it is so.

But only *apparently*. Jainism does not order one to do or not to do something. It only points the way and indicates various steps and stages along the way. No one is compelled to do anything. Jainism has always stressed 'Yatha Shakti' (within one's power) and 'Vartamana Joga' (depending upon the circumstances). This takes the edge off all the strictness. You do what you want to do, at your pace, according to you capacity. To me this is not strict at all.

No one says that self-control is easy or fun. Not controlling our selves will lead us into real trouble. Our monkey-mind resents all our attempts to control it, and it makes us find faults with the religion. Only we are responsible for our ignorance, hypocrisy, and dogmatism. The religion has always been against these, so let us not blame Jainism for them.

Now we know about the principles and practice of Jainism, and how that practice has affected the Jains and the rest of the world. That is the domain and the kingdom of Jainism, the sphere of influence of the word of the great Jinas, who conquered the hearts of the whole world, just by conquering themselves. Let us now meet the Jinas and their disciples, and other Jains great and small. While we are looking at the story of the Jinas and the Jains, we will also go over a few other stories to illustrate the point of Jinas' word.

In part III there will be all stories. In a democratic religion like Jainism, an authority is only as big as the arguments and points it presents. Having seen all the points and arguments, we are now ready to meet the ultimate Knowledge and the Truth, that is, the Jinas.

 END PART   II.

JAINISM   III

PROPHETS,   PUPILS   AND   PEARLS

1. JINAS AND ILLUSTRIOUS JAINS

In part I, we talked about the fundamental principles of Jainism, and in doing so, we learned to look at ourselves and the world around us in a new and different way. We travelled into our innermost space and got to know the Atma, and that our Atmas are no different from those of the great souls like the Jinas.

Part II traced the journey our soul undertakes to be one with the great souls. We looked at a few practical physical, mental and spiritual exercises to help us achieve that goal. We also looked at Jainism's festivals, and the influence it exerted over the world by its various contributions.

Although we went to an Upashraya and to the Derasara to worship the idol of the Lord, we did not get to meet the Tirthankaras. There are several reasons why we didn't. Without knowing what you know now, you wouldn't have been able to appreciate the greatness of the Tirthankaras, and their great blessings.

Also, even if you heard or read their life stories, you would have been at a loss in understanding why they did what they did. Moreover, you wouldn't have believed that they started out just as you and I are today. Lastly, you probably would want to know who speaks and spreads their word today.

In this third part, we will get to know the Tirthankaras and their great disciples who wrote down the Jinas' word, preserved it and explained it to us by their writings and by their own lives. We will also meet some of the great Acharyas who elaborated on the holy scriptures and who carried them into every village and every household, and into every heart.

We will also meet some of the noble-hearted Shravaks and Shravikas whose lives showed us how we can follow the Jinas' teachings without giving up our household and our loved ones.

Then we will go over a few fascinating stories. Jains are very good story-tellers. These stories are fantastic, but I should tell you something about them. Like gift wraps, they are very inviting and appealing, and they look fantastic under a Christmas tree. But the real gifts are inside. You have to go through the wrapping to see the gift within it. Just like

Aesop's fables, or the stories of Panchatantra, these stories also have a point to make, or some moral to convey. But there is more to this.

What really makes these stories and just about everything else with Jainism interesting, is that more you think about it, the more you get out of it. Like the Russian dolls, the more you look inside the more dolls you will find. When I say look 'inside', I do not mean only inside the stories. I mean to say 'within yourself' as well. These stories are not outside, they are not 'their' stories. They are *our* stories, and they are taking place within us.

Let me remind you of a couple of examples. When we talked about the fourteen dreams (in part II) that Lord Mahavira's mother saw when he was conceived, we said that they are actually our dreams, and they remind us of the fourteen Virtue Stations. When we visited the temple, we said that the temple actually represents our body, and within that we want to keep the idol of our Lord. This is the kind of thinking I would urge you to use while reading this.

The word for story is **Varta**. Do not confuse this word with the similar one - Vrata - meaning 'a vow'. The former comes from the word Vartmana (we came across this word in 'Vartmana Joga' earlier) meaning the news, or what's happening. This is the kind of story you read in a newspaper, or even in a fictional novel. The other word for a story is **Katha**, from the root word Kath meaning 'to tell'. Kathak dance is used to tell stories. A Katha is a story used as a medium to give a hidden message.

The Ramayana and the Mahabharata, the two great Indian epics are Kathas. The Jain stories you will read are Kathas, not Vartas. So enjoy them, but do think about them. If you understand this, you would not find them to be weird, and you would have fewer questions like 'How did he know that?' If it sounds ridiculous, it is, until you think more about it. The more absurd it sounds, the more likely there is a hidden message there.

The same goes for some aspects of Jainism itself. Not everything will make sense. The faithful may agree blindly with everything that is written, without questioning it, just because it is the Jina's word. Actually, not thinking would be a violent act, because the whole idea is to make you think. You may not understand it, no one else may understand it, so you keep on trying. You may never understand it. But you cannot simply agree with it without understanding. You accept it, respect it, or whatever, but you cannot simply agree with it and then forget about it.

At the same time, you cannot reject it just because you don't understand it. If we do so, we will end up rejecting Einstein's Theory of Relativity, Quantum Mechanics, or everything that's written in Sanskrit. You continue to work at it, think about it, and ruminate over it.

Jain Geography, Jain time-cycles (we did not talk about these two), the Tirthankaras and why there are twenty four of them, why there were many such twenty-foursomes in the past and will be as many more in the future, all defy simple logic, and scientific observations.

All we can do is apply Jinas' own principle of the Multiplicity of Viewpoints to the Jinas' own word (as we can get it), and very respectfully and faithfully try to understand it. We have all the time in the world. We know that they themselves had nothing to gain by writing these things. They were doing it for us. It is a will giving us our heritage and treasure. We may someday be able to decode it.

2. THE STORY OF JAINISM

Jainism as practiced today was 'started' by Lord Mahavira who was born in India more than 2500 years ago. This is about 500 years before Jesus Christ and the dawn of Christianity, and about 1100 years before the prophet Muhammad and Islam.

Lord Buddha, who founded Buddhism, walked on this earth around the same time as Lord Mahavira, and in the same State of Magadha (near today's city of Calcutta). We do not know whether these two great souls ever met, but the Buddhist scriptures do describe the event when Lord Buddha received the news of the death of Lord Mahavira.

INDIA BEFORE LORD MAHAVIRA

All of India was Hindu back then. We do not know who actually founded Hinduism. The Aryan tribes came from somewhere and settled in Europe, in Persia (today's Iran), and in India, several thousand years before Lord Mahavira. From the original Indo-European language, several European languages, Persian in Iran, and Sanskrit in India, came about. The Hindu Books of knowledge, the 'Vedas' (Ved = to know), and the epics the Ramayana and the Mahabharata are all in Sanskrit.

The Aryans mixed with the aborigine Indian natives called the Dravids, and a cultural assimilation took place. The southern Indian languages, viz., Tamil, Telugu, Kannada and Malayalam are Dravidian languages. The Northern Indian languages, viz., Gujarati, Marathi, Hindi, Punjabi, Bengali, etc. are Aryan, and hence, are derived from Sanskrit.

There were some intermediate forms of languages between Sanskrit and Gujarati, Marathi, and Hindi. In the State of Magadha, there were two such languages called Pali and Ardha-Magadhi (Ardha = half, semi-). Pali is the language of the Buddhist scriptures, while the Jain scriptures are in Ardha-Magadhi.

There were several democratic independent City States, like those of early Greece. The people ruled, the decisions were made in various assemblies, and in a few, there was an elected ruler, called a king. Magadha was such a State.

These kings and the people with whose consent they ruled were very independent people. But when it came to matters of religion and spirituality, whether it be the birth of a prince, starting ploughing the fields, marching the armies, offering prayers, or crowning a king, they were at the mercy of the court priest.

The reason being that all the Hindu scriptures were in Sanskrit, which only the high caste Brahmin priest could understand. Only the Brahmins were permitted to know and study Sanskrit, and to conduct ceremonies and worships. Therefore, in the minds of the people of the democratic states, there was a great deal of resentment towards the undue power of the priest. All the warriors, business people, and servants and workers did not amount to much.

Also, these Brahmin priests conducted animal sacrifices for their kings so that the latter could gain entry to heaven, beget a son, get a kingdom, or a bridegroom for their daughters. The sacrifices were for God or for the gods of rain, or water, or fire, and so on.

Many of these points are discussed very well in the excellent book 'Aapano Vaibhav Ane Varaso' (in Gujarati), by Mr. Manubhai Pancholi, 'Darshak' to whom my thanks are gratefully acknowledged here.

Jainism and Buddhism, both were born as a revolt against this Brahmin tradition, thereby accounting for their democratic structure and their stand against the killing of animals or anything else for that matter. Long before Lord Mahavira, as opposed to the Brahmana (In English it is *Brahmin*, but the original Sanskrit word is *Brahmana*) tradition, there was a Shramana tradition which was against animal sacrifices, and which emphasized the cultivation (*Shrama* = effort) of body and the mind towards salvation, and freedom from desires, rather than appeasing some gods to satisfy those ever increasing desires.

Both Jainism and Buddhism were largely ignored by the Brahmins, initially. Subsequently, there was a fierce animosity between them, and later on, between the Jains and the Buddhists as well. At one time, the Brahmins used to say 'Even if one is being chased by a mad elephant, one should not enter a Jain temple to find protection'.

Buddhism took a hold first over northern India, while Jainism spread first predominantly to the south and then northward to come to Gujarata on the west coast, which is the main center of Jainism today. About one thousand years ago, the great Hindu scholar and saint Shankara (Shrimad

Adi Shankaracharya) effectively wiped out Buddhism and Jainism from India. Jainism survived in Gujarata, Rajasthana, Maharashtra (around Bombay) and Bengal (around Calcutta). Buddhism practically disappeared from India, but it took hold in China, Japan, Thailand, Burma, SriLanka, Korea, Cambodia, and so on.

Fortunately, Indian tradition forgets and forgives history also. It is not uncommon for institutions led by Jains to install a statue of Shankaracharya. As relics of the old bad feelings among these three religions, a few curse words survive even today, and these are used without any sense of history by the followers of all these religions. These minor curses are part of the regular vocabulary. Only the Gujarati masculine versions are given below.

Bamano or Bhamato	A beggar.	Brahmins depended on society for their livelihood.
Luchcho	'Jain'. Cunning, or deceit-ful. Many Jains are money lenders, and some of them must have been loan sharks. Very violent indeed!	From 'Lunchan' or the Jain monks' pulling out the hairs from their own heads.
Budhdhu	Ignorant, innocent, dimwit. A Budhdhist!	Lord Buddha paid more attention to the practice of religion, rather than to the philosophy of the soul, etc. So, a 'Budhdhu' is one who does not understand any philosophy ('or anything else').

From this historical background, it is easy to understand the democratic nature of Jainism. Once the high-caste Brahmins were out, all the others became equal. All eleven Ganadharas (early disciples) of Lord Mahavira were Brahmins, and we are thankful to them for our scriptures.

It became clear that even if God is the creator, He cannot be pleased if we kill the animals that were created by Him. If it is improper to kill them for the Lord, then it is improper to kill them for our food also. Thus, Vegetarianism was born. One would not be surprised to know that all the Tirthankaras were born in Kshatriya (warrior) King families, rather than in Brahmin families.

JAINISM TODAY

Today, Jains are mainly business people from Gujarata (Ahmedabad), Maharashtra (Bombay), Rajasthan, and Bengal (Calcutta). They are leaders in business, especially the diamond market. These businesses employ many people. The Jains build schools, hospitals, temples, libraries and so on. They have been the money lenders to kings and to governments.

Jains are India's small but powerful and highly influential community. There are more than five million Jains out of 850 million people in India. This amounts to less than 1 percent, but it is still a large number. There are now more than five million Buddhists in India, thanks to the so-called 'untouchables' who converted to it. This is like a re-birth of Buddhism. Although, theoretically Jainism is not against the untouchables, Jains have stayed on the side lines on this important issue.

The first generation immigrants who came to the United States were professionals and from well to do families, far from being 'the poor, tired, huddled masses'. A great number were from Gujarata, and many of them were Jains. Jain temples have started appearing on the U.S. landscape. There are 57 Jain Centers in various cities in the U.S. And today there are about 75,000-100,000 Jains living here.

The second generation Jains are growing up now. They are interested in knowing about their religion, but there are very few monks and other sources of information. This generation is not well conversant with Gujarati, Hindi, or Sanskrit. The books about Jainism written in English are meant for the western readers who at least know Christianity or Judaism. At this writing, educational materials and a core curriculum are being developed.

Jainism has helped hundreds of generations to live good lives, and has survived all kinds of attacks. Whether it survives migration and implantation in this foreign soil is entirely in the hands of the second and subsequent generations, for whom this book is specially written. May the Jinas bless them!

3. TIRTHANKARAS

LORD MAHAVIRA

Lord Mahavira is the 'founder' of Jainism as it is practiced today. As you remember, one who founds the four part Sangha or Tirtha (a dock) is called a Tirthankara. Lord Mahavira or Mahavira Swami (Swami = a master) is the twenty fourth Tirthankara. Instead of only one founder, the Jain tradition believes in many Tirthankaras that occurred in the past, and many more to come in the future, none in our life-time though. The most recent or the 'current' twenty-four Tirthankaras span several thousand years. We will look at the lives of five Tirthankaras.

Mahavira (Maha = great, Vira = victor) was born in Magadha, to king Siddhartha and his queen Trishala. When Mahavira was to be born, mother Trishala saw Fourteen Dreams including an elephant, the moon, the sun, and other very auspicious things. She saw them shine very brightly. We already talked about these dreams in the second part.

In the morning, she reported this to the king who then summoned the scholars to his court. They analyzed her dreams very carefully and proclaimed that the queen was to deliver a son who will illuminate the whole universe.

As tradition has it, a Brahmin woman named Devananda also had seen the dreams come but then they vanished. The unborn child Mahavira was removed from her womb and was planted in mother Trishala's womb by the devas (gods, the 'shining ones'), since no Tirthankara can be born to a Brahmin woman. The reason for this is understandable from the discussion in the previous chapter.

When Mahavira was born, all the gods and their king Indra came and took the child to the top of the Mount Meru and held an Abhisheka (meaning bathing and worshipping). Indra had some doubts whether this child was really a great one. Mahavira who was born with the knowledge of all books, inherent sense and wisdom, and the knowledge of what's happening (Shruta Gnyana, Mati Gnyana and Avadhi Gnyana), saw this and pressed his right great toe against Mount Meru and the entire mountain started shaking. Indra got the message, and continued to pay his respects.

Indra's wife Indrani (Indra and Indrani are titles, not their names) had her own doubts. The child was so white and beautiful, that she wondered whether all that whiteness was due to the milk-like waters of the Kshira Samudra (Milk Sea) used for the ceremony. She kept on rubbing Mahavira's forehead with the end of her sari to convince herself, and finally she was!

Since Mahavira's birth, his father saw wealth, peace, prestige, crops, and everything else increase, therefore he named the child Vardhamana ('Incremental'). Vardhamana grew up, went to school even though he had nothing left to learn from there. He then married a lovely woman named Yashodhara and had a child from her.

But his mind was not in these worldly things. He was upset by all the unhappiness of the people all around him. After his parents died, he respectfully asked his elder brother to look after the kingdom and to let himself leave them so that he could set out in search of peace and happiness for the world.

His brother asked him not to leave so soon after their parents' death. Vardhamana stayed but continued to give up all his possessions to the poor. Finally he left the Sansara (worldly business), and left the palace barefoot, with no money, no servants, no companions, nor his wife, with only one piece of clothing that he was wearing. He left everything behind, everything that ordinary people will die or kill someone, to acquire.

The cloth got torn, so he gave away one half of it to someone. Later on he discarded the remaining part also. Then after retreating to the forest, he removed all the hairs from his head with his hands. Then he sat in meditation. He would fast for days, weeks, and months at a time, then eat for one day and start again.

He suffered greatly. Once a cowherd asked him to look after his cows, but Vardhamana, deep in his meditation (Kayotsarga or Kausagga) did not hear him. When the cowherd came back and did not see his cows, he became very furious and he pushed some nail-like sharp objects into Vardhamana's ears. Yet, Vardhamana did not move.

All Tirthankaras are born with three (Mati, Shruta and Avadhi) Gnyanas. When Vardhamana gave up his clothes and his hairs to take a vow of monkhood (called 'Diksha' or Initiation) he attained the fourth Gnyana (Manah-Paryava Gnyana, or being able to read other people's mind). After many years of Tapa, twelve and a half years to be exact,

Vardhamana attained the pure knowledge —Kevala Gnyana, which is the fifth and the highest Gnyana.

On reaching Kevala Gnyana, he became the Arihanta, or Jina whose enemies were conquered. He proved himself to be a great victor over himself, so he came to be known as Mahavira from then on. He then started preaching to give benefit of his knowledge to others. All the people and animals found his speech like a soothing balm on their burning wounds. So, many of the listeners followed him and became his disciples.

His eleven Ganadharas (main disciples) were Brahmins. They organized and wrote down his teachings later on for us. This twelve part compendium is called **Dvadashangi** (Dvi = two, Dasha = ten, Anga = body parts, that is 'in twelve parts').

Vardhamana left the Sansara at age 30, became Mahavira at age 42, and he achieved Nirvana (died) at age 72 years, on the last day of the Hindu year, leaving the illuminated path of liberation for the world behind.

He was never angry with anyone, even with those who inflicted pain on him. He felt sorry even for those who would hurt him. He was full of love for all people and animals. He cared for his family, but for such great souls the whole universe is their family. They are so big, their 'self' includes all of us. Today, 2500 years later, he is survived by five to six million Jains.

ADISHVARA BHAGAVANA

Lord Mahavira was the 24th Tirthankara. The first Tirthankara was Adishvara. Adi = first (similar to 'Adam' the first man), Ishwara = Bhagvana = the Lord. Lord Adishvara is also known as Rushabha Deva, Rushabha is a bull or an ox, Deva = god, the shining one. Adishvara preceded Lord Mahavira by thousands of years.

Before going further, I should tell you that the words Swami (master), Natha (master), Deva (god, the shining one), Bhagavana (the one who brings us fortune), Ishwara (who commands everything) are synonyms, and you may see one or more of these used in connection with the Tirthankaras, and other respectable people.

Adishvara was a very tall person, about 500 yards, we are told. He was truly a great man. In his days, people did not know how to build houses, or how to raise crops. Brothers and sisters used to marry. In other words, there was no civilization. He started it.

He did a lot of Upavasas and other Tapas, and he achieved Kevala Gnyana, and 'started' Jainism. He had illustrious sons Bharat and Bahubali, plus 98 more, and had two daughters. The Lord's mother Maru Devi could be proud of them all. We will take a look at the story of Maru Devi, the Lord's Mother, and the story of the Lord's two sons later on.

Once the Lord did Upavasa for more than a year. People in those days did not quite know, what can be offered to a Sadhu. Finally, his great-grandson claimed that honor by offering sugar-cane juice. Even today, a Tapa lasting longer than a year, called Varashi Tapa (Varasa or Varsha = a year), consisting of Upavasa and Ekasanu is ended with a Paranun of sugar-cane juice.

Sometimes, with a Tapa, one can also take a vow to end the Tapa only when certain kind of food is offered under certain conditions. One word about this vow or **Abhigraha**. They are not announced to the world. The Tapasvi (one who does the Tapa) keeps that in his or her mind and continues the Tapa until the vow is satisfied. You wouldn't ask me about cheating on these vows, right? Well, no one forces anybody to take the vow anyway. You can take a closed vow, that you will wait for only so long, then you will end the Upavasa regardless.

NEMI NATHA

Lord Nemi Natha is the 22nd Tirthankara, and he was a cousin of Lord Krishna. Nemi Natha was to marry the princess Rajimati, commonly known as Rajul. Her father had prepared for a big wedding, and as was the custom then, he had gathered many animals who were to be slaughtered and fed to the wedding party.

When the bridegroom, with his knowledge (remember, Tirthankaras are born with three Gnyanas?) saw and heard the shrieks of these animals, he thought that all of them would be saved if he refused to get married. Indeed, he did so, and went into a forest, did severe Tapa and attained Kevala Gnyana.

PARSHVA NATHA

Parshva Natha is the 23rd Tirthankara, after Nemi Natha and before Mahavira Swami. You may know him as the Bhagavana with a snake-hood over his head. There may be none, one, or more, upto a thousand (small) hoods. Look carefully the next time you go to the Derasara. The story of Parshva Natha is the story of why there is such a hood. This is the final reminder not to take these Kathas (with a deeper meaning) as Vartas (actual or fictional stories).

Before becoming Parshva Natha, he was a prince called Parshva Kumara. Once he was riding his horse and was going around inspecting his kingdom. He saw a man sitting in the hot sun with fires lighted all around him. The man explained that he was trying to please the gods with this 5-fire Tapa (four fires around him, plus the sun).

The prince could see that in one of the logs the man was about to toss into the fire, there was a snake, which the man had not noticed. Parshva Kumara told him to do as he pleased, but to spare the snake. The religious man got angry.

Many years later, when Parshva Natha was doing the Upavasa and other Tapa, and was standing in Kayotsarga and meditation, it started raining and it went on for days and nights. Everything was flooded. The water came upto Parshva Natha 's nose. He could see that Kamatha, that religious man had become a rain god and was taking out his anger on Parshva Natha after all these years.

Then suddenly Parshva Natha was lifted up by a creature, and was lifted up more and more as the water rose. The snake saved by the Lord had become the king of snakes and was helping Parshva Natha against torrential rains and floods by lifting him up and protecting the Lord's head with his hood.

What is more important is that Parshva Natha continued to meditate. He was neither too pleased with the snake - Dharanendra, nor was he angry with Kamatha. To him there was no friend, no foe. His mind was so balanced. He had conquered his likes and dislikes. He was a Jina.

MALLI NATHA

Lord Malli Natha, or the nineteenth Tirthankara was a woman. Very few religions give equal treatment to women. Jainism does. Like all other Tirthankaras, she was also born in a Kshatriya family. Kshatriyas are protectors of knowledge, property and the herds of animals. They protect the cows and Brahmins and give up their own lives to protect them. No wonder Jinas are born in Kshatriya families.

In one of her previous births, Malli Kumari had done a few Upavasas with her friends. When her friends were ready to break the fast with a Paranun, Malli Kumari deceived them and fasted longer. That made her be born as a woman, but she did become a Tirthankara nonetheless.

Women in India have suffered a lot (like women everywhere else), making them and others believe that some bad Karmas on their part in their earlier births may have caused them to be born as women and suffer. The idea is not that women are bad or inferior, but that they suffer, and we have no good reason for it. Jainism understands that.

OTHER TIRTHANKARAS

We looked at the lives of the first, the 19th, and then the 22nd, 23rd and 24th Tirthankaras. There are other Tirthankaras whose names indicate the moon (Chandra Prabhu, Prabhu = Lord, master), religion (Dharma Natha), peace (Shanti Natha), modesty (Nami Natha), a lotus flower (Padma Prabha), victory (Ajita Natha), etc.

In all, there are 24 Tirthankaras. All these 24 Tirthankaras as a group are called a **Chauvisi** (Twenty-Foursome. Chau = four, Visa = twenty). In the Samayika, and Pratikramanas, it is customary to remember and pay respect to the Chauvisi. Just to remind you, there were many such Chauvisis and there will be many more.

The dates of the Tirthankaras' conception, birth, Diksha (renunciation of the worldly affairs), Kevala Gnyana, and Moksha (death) are important. These five holy events are called **Kalyanakas**. Jain scriptures record these dates for all Tirthankaras with a great deal of precision.

When you or your parents may not know the exact time of your birth, and when scholars cannot place Lord Mahavira historically in a particular exact year, such precise information about all Kalyanakas of all 24 Tirthankaras should raise a red flag, making us think more about it.

Maybe, by 24 Tirthankaras and their Kalyanakas we are to understand some state of the Atma, we don't know. Let us leave that open. For us, all Tirthankaras are same. Their number one, or sixteen or twenty two is not at all important. There is no hierarchy.

When you go to a Derasara, look carefully below the feet and legs of a Murti (idol). On the base there is usually the figure of a lion, or an ox, or other things. That tells you whose Murti it is supposed to be. A lion indicates Lord Mahavira, an Ox indicates Rushabha Deva (Adishvara), and so on. For Parshva Natha there is a snake, but you won't have to look at the bottom (it is there too), because it is right there over the Lord's head as a hood. These symbols are called **Lanchhanas** ('a blemish') for the reason that is not clear.

If Tirthankaras represent different stages of advancement of the soul, then Lanchhans may represent its weak point at that level. Some consider the word 'Lanchhana' to mean simply 'a sign' serving to identify an idol. The scholars are still divided on this issue. Maybe one of the readers of this book will figure this out. You are as capable of this as anybody else.

4. CONTEMPORARIES OF TIRTHANKARAS

MOTHER MARU DEVI

Maru Devi was the mother of Adi Natha or Rushabha Deva, the first Tirthankara. When the Lord achieved his Kevala Gnyana and started preaching the religion, mother Maru Devi felt very proud. She couldn't control her extreme happiness. She mounted on the royal elephant, and with all her entourage she went to where Rushabha Deva was preaching.

From a distance she saw her son whom she expected to see her and to come running to her and to fall at her feet in reverence. Her son Rushabha Deva did see her. But he had given up all worldly attachments, and all creatures small and big were equal to him. Therefore, Rushabha Deva continued to preach.

Maru Devi was disappointed and saddened. But she started thinking, and soon she saw that her son now belonged to the whole world, and he was fulfilling his mission. In doing that he was illuminating the world with enlightenment, and was adding luster to her name also.

She deeply regretted her being disappointed and repented for her mistake. In doing so, right there while sitting on the elephant, she reached the Kevala Gnyana. The elephant symbolizes pride (among other things) and it appears in the next story also.

BAHUBALIJI

Lord Rushabha Deva had 100 sons and two daughters. When he relinquished the worldly business and took a Diksha (vow to be a monk), he left his kingdom to his sons Bharat and Bahubali.Except Rushabha Deva's second son Bahubaliji (Bahu = the upper limbs, arms; Bala = Power. Bali = strong. Ji is an ending to show respect, e.g., Gandhiji, Rushabha Devaji, etc.), the rest of their brothers and sisters took Diksha as well and followed the Lord.

Now, Bharat needed to take over Bahubali's territory to proclaim himself a Chakravarti or an emperor. Bahubali did not yield. Bharat used a missile which was ineffective against a blood relative. That infuriated Bahubali. A fierce duel took place.

Bharat was a good and tough fighter. But he was no match to Bahubali, and was soon knocked down. To finish him off, Bahubali raised his right hand and made a fist. Suddenly he thought, 'Why am I doing this? To kill my brother, who rightfully inherited the kingdom, and to be an emperor? Is it worth it? To be an emperor of a kingdom which my father gave up, and, my brothers and sisters would not touch either!'

Right then and there he decided to become a Sadhu. He lowered his fist just slightly and pulled off his hairs as all monks do at the time of their Diksha. He stood right there in Kayotsarga, and fasted for many days. Everybody knew that he will achieve Kevala Gnyana any minute. But he did not. His two sisters, who had become nuns, went to the Lord and asked him why their brother was not achieving Kevala Gnyana.

The Lord explained that Bahubali had decided to become a monk but he did not join his brothers; for, even though he was elder to them, his brothers were senior in the Sangha since they had taken the Diksha before he did. Therefore, he would have to offer respect and service to them. He gave up the kingdom to his elder brother, now he will have to serve the younger ones. His pride would never let him do that.

The sisters went to where Bahubali was standing in deep meditation. They walked around him three times to offer respect (because he was about to get the Kevala Gnyana), and started singing, 'O our dear brother, get off the elephant. There can be no Kevala Gnyana on top of an elephant'.

Bahubali heard this, and recognized the voices, but he could not make sense of the song. He was very smart too. He started thinking and soon figured it out. He was too proud! That was the elephant! He saw his mistake, and started repenting for that, and he promptly achieved the Kevala Gnyana.

Maru Devi was sitting on an elephant, yet she attained the Kevala Gnyana. Bahubali was not on a real elephant but he could not get the Kevala Gnyana. It is pride, ego and our vanity that block our way. Today, in southern India, near Bangalore, at Shravana Belagoda ("the monks' lake"), there is an approximately fifty seven foot tall statue of Bahubaliji, known as **Gomateshvaraji** which you may like to visit. It is on top of a small hill.

SHRENIKA RAJA

King Shrenika of Magadha is known in history as King Bimbisara. Jain literature knows him as Shrenika Raja ('Raja' means 'a king'). He was a great devotee of Lord Mahavira. Shrenika's virtuous and brilliant son Abhaya Kumara is also well known. There are many interesting stories about them.

One day Lord Mahavira was giving a discourse, and Shrenika, his son Abhaya Kumara and others were sitting. A god appeared there and told the Lord, 'Mahavira, you should die'! Before angry Shrenika could say anything, the god told him, 'Shrenika, you should stay alive'. Then he told Abhaya Kumara (Abhaya = fearlessness) to either live or die, and then he told the town butcher, who was sitting there, neither to live nor to die. When asked by the King about these strange statements, the Lord explained.

'O Shrenika! When I die, I will be a free soul. So the god wished me death. You are a good king, but a king is responsible for the Papas of his people, and they are a plenty. It is better for you to stay alive, becausewhen you die, you will go to hell, for quite some time'.

'Abhaya Kumara is virtuous and helpful when he is here, and when he dies he will go to heaven. So, he can choose either. For this butcher, he will keep on killing and accruing Papas while he is alive, and because of his sinful life thus far, when he dies, he is going to go to the seventh hell. It is bad for him either way'.

Even apparently annoying statements can reveal the truth in some way. Therefore, the Lord preached tolerance toward all view points. One should try to understand the deeper and the real meaning of what is said, rather than giving an angry, knee-jerk reaction.

THE KING PRASANNA CHANDRA

Chandra means the moon, and Prasanna means 'pleased' or 'happy'. The king's name means 'full moon', which gives cool light. His story indicates the effect of our thinking just as was the case with Maru Devi and with Bahubalji.

Prasanna Chandra gave up his kingdom, crowning his child prince as king. He became a monk and did a lot of Tapas. Once, King Shrenika, on his way to Lord Mahavira's sermon, passed by Prasanna Chandra and was impressed by his severe Tapa.

Shrenika asked Lord Mahavira what fate will befall that monk king. The Lord said 'He will go to the first hell,....no, the second...no..no...the seventh hell'. King Shrenika could not believe his ears. So he asked again. The Lord said, 'He will go to the first heaven, no.. no....Seventh heaven. No, wait!' Then they heard the gods celebrating & rejoicing. Shrenika Raja (King) looked at the Lord, who said 'Prasanna Chandra just attained the Kevala Gnyana'. Shrenika requested the Lord to explain all this, and the kind and the merciful Lord obliged.

The Lord said, 'Prasanna Chandra was meditating, but then he heard some passers by talking about how his kingdom was attacked by the enemies and how the child king couldn't fight them back. On hearing that, the monk got very angry. In his mind, he put on armor and started killing his enemies. He felt more and more violent.

'Finally, he found the enemy king and knocked him down, and to smash the fallen king's head with the headgear of his own armor, Prasanna raised his hand and touched his own head. That is when, O Shrenika, I told you that he would go to the seventh hell'.

'When Prasanna touched his head devoid of any hairs, he realized that he had slipped badly from his meditation. He felt endless remorse and felt repentant. He kept on repenting more and more and then he finally attained Kevala Gnyana. O Shrenika, so great is the power of our thoughts'.

THE SNAKE CHANDA KAUSHIKA

Once Lord Mahavira was going from town to town and he had to cross a forest. The town people urged him not to go that way, because there was a fierce snake there who had killed many people. Mahavira was not afraid. He went there. The snake promptly came out and as expected, bit the Lord on his foot.

From the Lord's foot some fluid started oozing, but it was not blood. It was milk, the proverbial food and drink for snakes. Startled and puzzled, the snake looked up. He saw no anger in those moist eyes full of compassion. He heard the calm, soothing words, 'O Chanda Kaushika, won't you ever understand? Learn, Chanda Kaushika, learn!'

Chanda Kaushika's whole life, full of anger and venom, flashed in front of him. With the Lord's blessing he could see his previous births, in one of which he was a great monk. He used to do a lot of Tapa. Once on the way back to the Upashraya, he accidentally stepped on a frog and killed it.

One of his very young disciples saw this, and several times reminded him to seek forgiveness for that. With one more reminder, Chanda ('angry') Kaushika's volcano erupted. He ran after the young disciple who was too quick for him. In the darkness of the Upashraya the Guru Chanda Kaushika hit his head against a pillar and died instantly. Still full of anger, he was eventually reborn as a fierce snake!

The milk oozing out of the Lord's wound, signifies his love and mercy. That, and the Lord's telling Chanda Kaushika to understand and learn, opened his eyes completely. The message was clear. 'Chanda Kaushika, you were great, and you still are, but your anger overpowers you. Your anger has made you a furious snake, avoided by everybody. And yet, you are not giving up your anger. Even I, Mahavira, am not spared by you. Chanda Kaushika, if not now, when, O when would you learn to control your anger? Learn to forgive. Forgiveness, born out of love and compassion, is the best remedy for anger'.

The snake, once the great monk Chanda Kaushika, saw the light and with deep repentance, eventually reached salvation. The Lord's mercy extends even to the lowliest and the most dangerous of all the animals.

5. DISCIPLES OF LORD MAHAVIRA

GAUTAMA SWAMI

Now let us continue our journey through history and meet some of Lord Mahavira's disciples and their descendents. Jainism's banner has been carried by them. It is only through them that the word of all the Tirthankaras has come down to us. It is their blessing bestowed upon us. Let us meet them.

Once there was a big Yagna going on in a town. Yagna is an ancient Vedic ritual of making offerings into the holy fire to please the gods. Eleven Brahmins were conducting the ceremonies. They were the best ones around and many people were expected to attend the Yagna. The eldest Brahmin priest was Indrabhuti, followed by his two brothers Agnibhuti and Vayubhuti and others. They saw throngs of people coming towards them, but the people did not stop at the Yagna. They continued to walk past the site to another place.

On inquiring, Indrabhuti learned that people were going to listen to Lord Mahavira who was preaching nearby. When no one was left at the Yagna site, Indrabhuti told his brothers, 'Let me go and take care of this new preacher. No one knows more than what we know. I will call his bluff, and be right back, meanwhile, you continue.'

Indrabhuti approached the place where Lord Mahavira was preaching. The Lord saw him from distance and said, 'Welcome, Indrabhuti'. Startled at first, Indrabhuti convinced himself that since he was so famous, it was no wonder this preacher knew his name. He nodded with pleasure.

'Indrabhuti, you have some doubts about the Atma. Let me explain', The Lord said. Indrabhuti and his brothers had several doubts, but their vanity prevented them from finding the right answers. The all-knowing Lord found this out, and solved Indrabhuti's doubts. Indrabhuti stayed as the Lord's disciple.

To make the long story short, one by one the other two brothers also came and became the Lord's followers. They were the first three of the eleven disciples who wrote down the Lord's teachings for us, in twelve parts called Dvadashangi (Dvadasha = twelve, Anga = part).

Indrabhuti came to be known as Gautama Swami. He is the first apostle or standard bearer of the religion. He is to Lord Mahavira, what St. Peter is to Jesus Christ. These apostles are called Ganadharas (Gana = a group, Dhara = to hold, to lead). Gautama Swami became Lord Mahavira's very intimate disciple and a friend. There are very many interesting dialogues between them. Some day you may want to read these.

When the time came for Lord Mahavira to leave this world and become a free soul, the Lord was worried. Gautama Swami was so attached to him, the Lord was concerned that his disciple would not achieve Kevala Gnyana. Attachment, even to the Lord, is not good.

The Lord dispatched Gautama to another town to answer some questions that one Brahmin had. A few days later when Gautama returned, Mahavira had already achieved Moksha. He was free from all the worldly bondage. Gautama was disappointed that the Lord had kept him by His side all His life, only to forsake him at the last minute. But Gautama was very learned and wise.

Just as Maru Devi Mata – Rushabha Deva's mother – had learned, Gautama also saw that it was not proper to cry. The Lord had given us knowledge and had showed us the path to our salvation. The Lord had sent Gautama away to spare him the agony. On thinking and understanding more and more, Gautama Swami achieved Kevala Gnyana.

Gautama Swami is not to be confused with Lord Buddha whose family name was also Gautama. Buddha's name was Siddhartha, which was also the first name of Mahavira's father. In addition, Buddha's wife was Yashoda, while Mahavira's wife was Yashodhara. No need to remember all this, but it is good to know.

I have used the word 'Buddha' rather than 'Budha', because the former is the right way to say it. The word means 'the enlightened one' (Budh = to know, and *Buddha* is part participle, for those of you who like the grammar). When Lord Mahavira confronted the snake Chanda Kaushika, the Lord told him, 'Chanda Kaushika, buza, buza (budh, budh)'. That is 'O Chanda Kaushika, learn, learn!'

CHANDANA BALA

'Chandana' means sandalwood, and 'bala' indicates a girl or a woman. Chandana Bala was a virtuous princess, spreading the fragrance of her virtues all around her. Her father's kingdom was taken over by Chandana Bala's mother's sister's husband. Chandana Bala escaped, but was caught by bad guys and was sold as a slave to the richest man in another town.

He was a businessman. Such businessmen are called 'Sheth', and the chief and richest of them in town, usually a powerful advisor and money-lender to the king, is called a 'Nagara Sheth' (Nagara = a city).

This Nagara Sheth was married, and he treated Chandana Bala as his daughter. Chandana Bala also treated him like her father. One hot after-noon, when the Nagara Sheth came home, Chandana Bala washed his hot feet with cool water in the courtyard. While she was doing so, her braids slipped and and fell in the muddy water. The Nagara Sheth casually picked that up with the other end of his walking stick, and moved her braids away from the mud. Neither he nor Chandana Bala gave this any further thought.

But the Shethani (Sheth's wife) saw all this from a window and got quite furious. When the Sheth was away on business, she took Chandana Bala, shaved off her head, put shackles on her hands and feet and put her in an out-of-the-way room. Chandana did not get anything to eat for three days. When Sheth came back, he hurriedly found some Bakula, which is simply soaked grains, from the house, and left to call a locksmith to open the shackles. Chandana Bala never liked to eat without first offering the food to monks.

This was her lucky day. She saw a monk, Lord Mahavira, approach-ing her. He had been fasting for five months and twenty five days. He was going from door to door but was not accepting any food. He had taken an *Abhigraha* (a vow) to accept food only when certain conditions were met. Chandana offered him the Bakula, he moved as if to accept. She was very much delighted. The Lord looked at her face and immediately started to walk away.

Chandana broke into tears. 'The Unlucky me! Even this much hap-piness I am not entitled to! What wrong have I done'? The Lord turned around and this time, he accepted the Bakula. The Lord of the universe who had turned down all other offers, accepted her worthless food!

Lord Mahavira had taken an Abhigraha to accept only Bakula, and that also, only when served by a princess whose head was shaven clean, who had shackles on her hands and feet, who was sitting astride a threshold, who had been fasting for three days, **and** who had tears in her eyes. The reason Lord Mahavira turned away the first time was, that her tears had disappeared on seeing Him. As soon as they reappeared, all the conditions were met.

The Lord is always looking for us, and is waiting to accept our offerings. But we have to meet certain conditions too. Only the Lord's mercy can help us meet him. The princess Chandana Bala later on became the first woman disciple of Lord Mahavira, and ultimately having reached Kevala Gnyana, found her liberation and became a Siddha.

6. DESCENDENTS OF THE LORD

BHADRA BAHU SWAMI

The eighth one to succeed Mahavira Swami and Gautama Swami was Bhadra Bahu Swami. He wrote several well known Sutras, the main one being the Kalpa Sutra, the best-known of Jain Books. It is read during the Paryushana, and it narrates the life of Lord Mahavira, and of the Gandharas. The Digambara sect began in Bhadrabahu's time. The story of Bhadra Bahu Swami's disciple Sthuli Bhadra's is fascinating.

STHULI BHADRA

In civilian life, Sthuli Bhadra was the son of the prime minister to the king. He fell in love with a beautiful courtesan Rupa Kosha ('treasury of beauty'). He left everything and went to live at her palace, and didn't even attend his father's funeral. When repentance set in, he became a monk.

To test the depth of Sthuli Bhadra's renunciation, and the strength of his character, the Guru permitted the monk Sthuli Bhadra to spend the four months of monsoon season at Rupa Kosha's palace. Sthuli Bhadra passed the test, he did not succumb to temtation. He lived with his once beloved treating her as a sister.

Sthuli Bhadra and Rupa Kosha have been the subjects of several dance dramas. Sthuli Bhadra is remembered more as Kosha's lover, rather than as Sthuli Bhadra Swami, but he was worthy in his own right.

Bhadra Bahu Swami had knowledge of the fourteen Purvas (from the 45 Agamas) and Sthuli Bhadra was sent to him by the Sangha to acquire that. Everything went well, and Sthuli Bhadra studied ten Purvas out of fourteen.

One day, Sthuli Bhadra's seven sisters came to see him. The Guru sent them to a cave where their brother had gone to meditate. The sisters went there but when they saw a lion in the place of their brother, they became frightened and returned to the Guru. Bhadra Bahu Swami calmed them down and asked them to go again. They went, and this time, met Sthuli Bhadra.

From then on, Bhadra Bahu Swami refused to teach him further. Sthuli Bhadra was not able to 'digest' the knowledge well. He was taught the way to take the form of a lion, etc. and he could not refrain from showing it off to his sisters, whom he frightened for no reason.

The Sangha intervened, and finally commanded Bhadra Bahu Swami to continue to teach Sthuli Bhadra. The Sangha has the final authority. So Bhadra Bahu did resume teaching, but only on the condition that Sthuli Bhadra would not teach it to anyone else. Thus Sthuli Bhadra was the last Sadhu to possess the knowledge of all of the fourteen Purvas.

You may have a problem with this story. Let me explain. Knowledge has to be passed on to the proper recipient. A Nuclear arsenal cannot be handed over to just anyone. Knowledge is not for showing off, or for harassing people. It is for helping them. Try to understand the message of the story. Read between and beyond the lines. Remember, all of these stories are Kathas.

Over the years, many of the religious Sutras were forgotten. The knowledge used to be preserved by word of mouth, and by memorizing and teaching to the next generation of monks. There wetre three meetings of Sadhus over subsequent hundreds of years. The last one was held in a town called Vallabhipura (the city of Vallabha). There they rewrote the scriptures from their collective memory, in forty five books called **Aagamas**. They are the Jain scriptures.

He was the one to preside over the first conference which gave us the Jain scriptures known as the Agamas. His Guru Bhadra Bahu Swami was away, and on returning, he disapproved of many of the Agamas and started the Digambara sect, which shares all the fundamental principles with other sects of Jainism.

HARI BHADRA SURI

'Suri' means an Acharya. In Hari Bhadra's time, there was animosity between the Jains and the Buddhists. One of Hari Bhadra's disciples was killed by some of the 1444 Buddhists in one place. Hari Bhadra took a vow to kill all 1444 of them by defeating them in a debate, with the condition that the loser would jump into boiling oil. Anger and violence get the better of us, and that happens to even the best ones, including the monks.

Hari Bhadra's Guru heard about this, and stopped him. He also imposed on him the penalty of writing 1444 Sutras. Hari Bhadra was very repentant, but Kevala Gnyana does not come as easily as it did in the time of Adi Natha and Mahavira Swami. No one gets it nowadays.

Hari Bhadra wrote 1440 Sutras (each stanza counts as one). Then he started to write the the one that begins with 'Sansara-davanala-daha-neerum--' which was to have four stanzas. This Sutra is unique, in that it contains no conjoined consonants (Jodakshara) so characteristic of Sanskrit writings. Someone in your family may be able to read that to you. The whole Sutra is reproduced in the Treasure Chest later on in this book.

Three stanzas of the Sansara-davanala-daha Sutra, or 1443 Sutras in all were finished, and the fourth and the last one was started. It is a prayer to the goddess of learning - Sarasvati. The first line was written. Then suddenly Hari Bhadra Suri died. The first line is a beautiful example of alliteration, where the 'L' sound is repeated eleven times.

The Sangha got together and wrote the last three lines to complete Hari Bhadra's penalty. Today also, in the Samvatsari and other major Pratikramanas, the whole Sangha sings these three lyrical lines as a chorus.

SIDDHASENA DIVAKARA SURI

In the Navakara Mantra, we say 'Namo Arihantanam, Namo Siddhanam...' etc. A great Acharya Siddhasena wrote only one line, translated in English as, 'I bow to Arihanta, Siddha, Acharya, Upadhyaya, and Sadhu' to cover the first five (out of nine) lines of the holy Navakara Mantra. That was the quickest and most efficient way to do that.

His Guru got annoyed with his fiddling with holy writings. This was not a question of efficiency or of saving time. Siddhasena should have thought more to find out why other brilliant people before him had not done that. Siddha Sena's 'Namorhat, Siddha....' Sutra is also used today, but never instead of the Navakara Mantra.

Siddhasena also wrote the most lyrical and very poetic 'Kalyana Mandira Stotra'. (Kalyana = Salvation, Mandira = a temple, an abode, Stotra = a Sutra of praise). This Stotra is written in praise of the Tirthankaras. You may like to have someone sing it to you and tell you its meaning. A couple of interesting stanzas from it are reproduced in the Treasure Chest later on. The Sutra is in Sanskrit. Siddhasena was a great scholar of Sanskrit.

His knowledge, his preachings and above all, his character impressed the local king so much that he would send a special escort to bring Siddhasena to his court. The escort would respectfully seat Siddhasena in a palanquin (like a rickshaw without wheels. It is carried by four people on their shoulders), and bring him there.

As you know there are several wrongs here. A Jain monk is not supposed to be in one place all the time. If the king wanted to listen to the Vyakhyana (a sermon) he should have gone to the Upashraya. Moreover, a monk should not use any vehicle, but should always walk, barefoot. Siddha Sena's Guru found this out, and was saddened.

One day, one of the regular palanquin-bearers couldn't come, so he sent a replacement, who was a rather old and feeble man. He couldn't carry the well-pampered body of Siddhasena, who soon got quite impatient. Palanquin is like an enclosed box with curtains on two sides. Siddhasena opened one curtain and asked the old man whether his shoulders were bothering him. He asked, in Sanskrit, 'Kim (what) tava (your) skandhe (in shoulder) badhati (does it hurt)?'

Note the similarity between the English 'To bother', and the Sanskrit 'Badh'. Anyway, the old man promptly replied in a soft voice, "Yes, it does hurt. But not as much as 'Badhati' does". Well, Siddhasena had used the wrong form of the verb. Instead of saying "Badhate" he had said 'Badhati'. So, the old man had said that he was more bothered by Siddha Sena's Sanskrit grammar than by his weight!

There weren't many people alive who could, or would dare to correct Siddhasena on a point like this. Siddhasena knew of only one person who could. He recognized the old palanquin bearer to be his Guru.

Immediately he fell to his Guru's feet and then walked back to the Upashraya with him.

Gurus are personifications of God. They are kind, merciful and forgiving. Even when we wander off the right path shown by them, they come looking for us to take us back. Knowledge is the least they give us. They also teach us modesty, keep us away from becoming proud, and show us how to be worthy of all the great things they teach us. Guru's position is higher than God, because it is the Guru who introduces us to God. That is the reason, in the Navakara Mantra, we say 'Namo Arihantanam' before saying 'Namo Siddhanam'.

MANATUNGA SURI

Like Siddha Sena's **Kalyana Mandira Stotra**, there is another beautiful and equally poetic **Bhaktamara Stotra** by Manatunga Suri. Both these form part of a group of nine Sutras which should be recited everyday in the morning. They are called **Nava** (nine) **Smarana** (to remember). The Navakara Mantra is the first one, and with these two Stotras we have a total of three.

In addition, Bhadra Bahu's Sutra called **Uvasagga-Haram** ('remover of obstacles') is also there. Then there are five more, including the **Great Peace Sutra**, and a prayer of Lord Ajita Natha and Lord Shanti Natha (2nd and 16th Tirthankaras, respectively). The **Ajita-Shanti Stotra** is very lyrical and it is a delight to hear someone sing it well. A sample from that is given in the Treasure Chest.

There is an interesting story about how Manatunga Suri's Bhaktamara ('Immortal Devotees') Stotra came about. Once a king was highly impressed by a Brahmin scholar who showed all kinds of miracles. The king then asked his Jain minister whether Jain monks were capable of doing any such things. The minister replied that indeed they are, but they stay away from such displays. Then he met his Guru Manatunga Suri who reluctantly agreed in the interest of the Jainism to show a miracle.

At his instructions, the king put forty eight shackles on the upper and lower limbs of the Suriji, and enclosed him behind forty eight doors. Manatunga Suri started composing the Bhaktamara Stotra which is a prayer to Adishwara, the first Tirthankara. The Stotra has 48 stanzas. As Manatunga Suri kept on creating stanza after stanza, one after the other doors kept on opening and shackles kept on breaking apart. The king was of course convinced.

Jains consider this Stotra to be very powerful and capable of bringing them all kinds of riches and other good things. But what riches can be worthier than the liberation of our Atma? This Stotra is capable of freeing us from all kinds of shackles that bind us, and no materialistic gain is to be asked for from it. If we do ask, we bind ourselves, and belittle the Stotra as well. Forty eight shackles are enough, why add more?

We will sample a few marvelous stanzas from the Bhaktamara and Kalyana Mandira Stotras later. We will also see a sampling of the works by other great monks we talked about. But no talks about monks can be called 'complete' without talking about Hema-chandr-acharya Suri.

ACHARYA SHRI HEMA-CHANDRA SURI

You know that Acharya and Suri signify the same. Shri shows respect. For Shravaks, 'Shri' is the same as 'Mister'. *Hema* means gold, and *Chandra* is the moon. Hemchandra shines like the full moon in the history of Jainism, that of Sanskrit literature and that of Gujarata and its literature. Hemachandra lived in the town called Patan (meaning the capital city) in Gujarata, during the golden age of that state, a little more than nine hundred years ago.

Hemachandra wrote innumerable Sutras, Stotras and manuscripts. He is the first one to write the grammar of the old Gujarati language when the latter had barely begun. There are very few subjects he did not write about. He wrote in Sanskrit, in Ardha–Magadhi and in early Gujarati.

Siddharaja Jaysinha was the king of Gujarata then. Hemachandra actively worked to protect and spread Jainism. He was influential with Siddharaja, and especially so with his successor Kumarapala, who officially adopted Jainism as his religion. It is thanks to the influence of Hemachandra and of his disciple King Kumarpala (of the Solanki Dynasty), that Gujarata is the main center of Jainism today.

Hemachandra was a prolific writer. Leaving the quality and the content of his writings aside, although both are superb, the sheer volume of his work appears to be a physical impossibility. One should remember that all this work is in poetry which has to be composed also. His works on poetry (Kavya-Anushasan) and on the Yoga (Yoga Shashtra) are well known. His grammar (Vyakarana) dedicated to King Siddharaja, called Siddha-Haima-Vyakarana (that is 'grammar of Siddharaja and Hemchandra') is also well known.

There were many other very well known great Acharyas and other monks. To name a few, Kundkund-Acharya, Shri Anand-Ghanaji, Shri Yasho-Vijayaji, and so on. Let us conclude this chapter by paying our respects and our thanks to all the Tirthankaras, their contemporaries, and all the great monks and nuns that we talked about, or omitted only because of limited space.

Namo Arihantanam.	(Arihanta)
Namo Siddhanam.	(Siddha)
Namo Ayarianam.	(Acharya)
Namo Uvazzayanam.	(Upadhyay)
Namo Loe Savva Sahunam.	(All Sadhus, monks)

7. A FEW GREAT SHRAVIKAS

Tirthankaras, other Jinas, and monks and nuns can write great books, preach high principles, do extreme degrees of Tapa, and guide the Sangha, but they are limited in actually doing anything material, like building temples, libraries, hospitals, or schools.

They do not bear children either. Therefore, the day to day religious practice depends on Shravaks and Shravikas. They can bear and educate children who can then transmit the faith to their children. It is also the Shravaks and Shravikas who become monks and nuns.

We should understand that being a monk or a nun is basically a state of mind, rather than just dressing or living in a particular way. Monkhood or nunhood is only a means of practicing the religion, but is not a pre-requisite. There are many Shravaks and Shravikas who have been able to uplift their souls to the highest level, while many monks and nuns have seen their own downfalls.

Without belittling the remarkable achievements of the monks and nuns, or implying any disrespect, it can be said that it is easier to take one-self out of all likes, dislikes, anger, passion, greed, and the whole Sansara, but it is far more difficult (and more desirable) to remove the Sansara from one's self. As you know, Maru Devi Mata and many others including the snake Chanda Kaushika were able to achieve salvation. Let us look at some great Shravikas.

It is said that a mother is equal to one hundred teachers. All the great men and women we talked about and will talk about, had their moth-ers bring them up properly, instil good values and virtues in their minds, and expose them to high thoughts and good people.

Also, we talked about the sisters of Bahubaliji, who helped him come down from the elephant of pride. Sthuli Bhadra's sisters' talking to his Guru (after seeing the lion in that cave), was an important event in Sthuli Bhadra's life.

Women on their own, as women, rather than as a mother, a sister, or a wife, have been great too. All the way from Maru Devi Mata, to Chandana Bala, down to today, there have been many great Shravikas. Sthuli Bhadra's beloved courtesan Rupa Kosha was no small woman. A woman can cause a man's downfall, or she could elevate him to lofty heights.

When Lord Nemi Natha (the 22nd Tirthankara, we went over his story earlier), felt mercy on animals which were to be eaten, he decided not to marry the princess Rajimati (or Rajula). But she later decided to follow him as a nun. Once, in a cave, she was approached by Nemi Natha's brother, who was also a Sadhu, who tried to seduce her. It was she who calmly talked to him, 'You are still interested in this body of mine, which your brother had spat out!' That brought him to his senses, and helped him continue on the right path.

There have been innumerable great Shravikas whose stories are not included here, because more than a passing acquaintance with Indian culture, and with Jainism, is required to appreciate the importance of their Kathas. Sulasa, Mrigavati, Damayanti, Subhadra, and many other gems are there, and you may request your teacher to tell you about them.

If you think women are under-represented here, they are. Wealth and power, and hence building temples or doing major charities have always been men's domain. But, women were always there, and without them nothing would have come about.

8. A FEW GREAT SHRAVAKS

SHREEMAD RAJCHANDRA

Shreemad Rajachandra is known only as Shreemad (Reverend) rather than as Rajachandra, which was his name. He lived in the later part of the nineteenth century. He never formally became a monk, but he studied and wrote a great deal, most of it poetry.

He was a poet, a teacher, and a guide. He died at a very young age, but even in his short life, he was able to uplift himself to such an extent that he is worshipped with great reverence. There are several institutions today that are devoted to his teachings.

He learned about Jainism from his mother and about Vaishnava (followers of Lord Vishnu) Hinduism from his grandfather. His deep study and thinking and his innate wisdom made him a Guru to many.

In his autobiography, Gandhiji writes a whole chapter on Rajachandra who was then known as Rayachandabhai. They had exchanged several letters when Gandhiji was in South Africa and was about to convert to Christianity. Before taking that step, Gandhiji formulated several questions and presented them to Rajachandra, who answered them in detail to Gandhiji's satisfaction.

Gandhiji did not convert, and then used principles of several religions to guide people of India to their political freedom. This struggle was non-violent. The influence of Jainism and of Shreemad Rajachandra was undeniable.

SHRI VIRACHANDA GANDHI

Not many Jains are familiar with this name, but they should be. Just about one hundred years ago, in Sept. 1893, The World Conference of Religions was held in Chicago. A young Hindu saint from India, Swami Vivekananda attended this, and dazzled the delegates and other listeners. This was an unforgettable event.

With Swami Vivekananda, there was a younger Jain Shravak named Virachanda Gandhi. Virchandabhai (Bhai = a brother) was only 29 years old then. He addressed the conference and informed the delegates about the principles of Jainism, the political and cultural condition of India under the British rule, and joined Vivekananda in defending against the attacks on Hinduism. He worked to dispel many misconceptions about India, without criticizing any of the other religions.

He made three trips to the United States before he died in 1901, at the young age of 37, and established several institutions in America. He authored several articles and books, viz. The Jain Philosophy, The Karma Philosophy, etc. He was of no relation to Mahatma Gandhi, but they did know each other.

VASTUPAL, TEJPAL & VIMAL SHAH.

These three great Shravaks were the chief advisors and ministers (administrative, not religious priests) to the various kings of Gujarata. Vastupal and Tejpal were brothers. Vimal Shah predates them by several hundred years. These great Shravaks built the marvelous temples of Delwada on Mount Abu in Rajasthana, a neighboring state of Gujarata.

These temples are carved out of marble and are beautiful examples of Jain art, architecture and sculpture. Vastupal and Tejpal's wives personally supervised the construction and looked after the workers. When you go to India, make it a point to see these temples.

Also note that the inner sanctum of these and other temples, where the Lord's idol is installed, is very plain and simple, without any elaborate carvings or decorations. You may drive a Rolls-Royce or a Mercedes to meet your friend, but you do not take it into his or her living room. A good temple just takes you to the Lord. But the Lord does not need any decoration. It is the Lord, and not the temple that is important.

JAGADU SHAH AND BHAMA SHAH

These two unrelated great Shravaks were rich men. Jagadu Shah gave up all his wealth, you cannot even imagine how much, to feed Gujarata during a major devastating famine.

Bhama Shah was a minister and friend to the king Pratap of Mevad in Rajasthana. Pratap fought the Muslim Moghul empire seated in Delhi, but several losses made him devastated and despondent. His children did not even have milk to drink. The king had no choice but to flee, which was worse than dying. The loyal minister Bhama Shah came to the rescue. He gave up his wealth so that king Pratap could continue to fight.

SHETH MOTI SHAH AND SHETH HATHI SINGH

These great Shravaks were both businessmen and during the last two hundred years, they built several beautiful temples in the holy city of Palitana, Ahmedabad, Bombay and in many other places. You may like to visit them.

BABU PANALAL

Panalal was a rich jeweler from Calcutta. In the nineteenth and the twentieth centuries he spent a lot of money in Bombay, and in many other places. He built an excellent high school (Babu Panalal Puranchand Jain High School) for Jain boys in Bombay, where this author was fortunate enough to study.

One of the students of that school, **Sheth Kantilal Ishwaralal** grew up to be a rich man and built another school, Shakuntala Kantilal Ishwarlal Jain Girls High School in Bombay. Either of your parents, or their friends may have studied in one of these schools.

There are innumerable temples, schools, libraries, hospitals, orphanages, animal shelters, and so many other forms of charities operated by many Shravaks and Shravikas whom history may not even know, but whose contribution no one can ignore or forget. That torch is now passed onto you. Keep it burning, and pass it along.

Now we are close to the modern times. In this 20th century, Jains have migrated to Africa, Middle East, Japan, Europe and the United States. Innumerable Jains have made tremendous contributions to preserve and propagate Jainism in these new lands. We will leave it for the future historians to acknowledge their contributions.

Jai Jinendra!

9. A FEW JAIN KATHAS

So far we have talked about real people, and their work. Now we will see some fictional stories with real messages. Don't get hung up on 'How is that possible?' kind of questions. Just try to understand the message.

SAVA SHETH AND SOMA SHETH

Business people are known as Shahs or Sheths. Sava Chanda and Soma Chanda were merchants. Both were very rich. They lived in different towns. They did not know each other personally, but they had heard each other's names.

Once, Sava Sheth ran into bad fortune and lost all his wealth in business. He could not even pay off the money he owed to other businesses, who demanded their money. Sava Sheth was desperate. No one could help him except possibly Soma Sheth, but he didn't even know him.

Sava Sheth picked up his pen, his hands shaking with nervousness and hesitation and wrote a money order to be paid by Soma Sheth. Such money order, called a 'Hundi' is like a bank check, and is written in the name of the person who owes you money. It was a bogus check, and was sure to bounce back. But Sava Sheth was desperate.

The creditors took the check, and after several days' journey, they reached Soma Sheth's town and presented the Hundi to Soma Sheth's accountant. The accountant was startled at first, on looking at the huge amount written in the Hundi. He was startled still more, to find no account in the name of any Sava Sheth in any of his books.

He took the Hundi to his boss Soma Sheth. The Sheth was also puzzled, but his sharp eyes saw a smudge on the Hundi. It looked like a water mark and the ink had run in that area. Recognizing that as a desperate tear from sad eyes, he told the accountant, 'Please pay this off. Sava Sheth is a close personal friend of mine, so there is no need to enter this into our books either.'

The story could have ended there, but it did not. Years went by, and Sava Sheth's fortune took another turn. He regained his wealth and much

132

more. But he was not the one to forget his debt to Soma Sheth who had honored his Hundi, even though they didn't even know each other. Sava Sheth took with him all the money he owed, plus the interest due, and came to the office of Soma Sheth.

After the initial formal greetings, Sava Sheth thanked Soma Sheth and requested him to take his money back. Soma Sheth said, 'I don't know what you are talking about! Our account books do not show any such transaction. I hardly even know you, except from your fame as a very wealthy businessman'. His accountant confirmed that there was no such amount outstanding in the name of Sava Sheth.

History has rarely been witness to such a dispute! Sava Sheth wouldn't keep the money, and Soma Sheth wouldn't take it. Finally, with the help of the Sangha, they decided to use that money to build a temple at Palitana. When you go there, you can see Sheth Sava-Soma's temple among nine temples known as Nava (nine) Tunks ('u' as in Put). We do not know who these Sheths were, or where and when they lived!

SHALI BHADRA

Shali Bhadra was a very rich young man, who lived in the city of King Shrenika, at the time when Lord Mahavira was alive. Shali Bhadra's father had accumulated and earned a lot of wealth. Shali Bhadra lived on the seventh floor of his palace with his thirty two beautiful wives, who were ready to fulfil any and every desire he could think of. Plus, there was an army of servants. After his father's death, Shali Bhadra's mother, Bhadra Shethani ran the day to day business. Shali Bhadra had no need to see the real world.

Once, a merchant came with a few pieces of very expensive fabric, woven in silver and gold, and studded with diamonds, rubies, and emeralds. He went to King Shrenika's palace, but the king could not afford to buy even one piece, so the merchant was very much disappointed. Someone then directed him to Shali Bhadra's palace.

Bhadra Shethani welcomed him and treated him nicely. Really rich people are never arrogant. The merchant then showed his fabrics. Bhadra Shethani asked him how many pieces he had. He said he had sixteen. Shethani bought all sixteen, and tore each piece into two, one for each of her thirty two daughters-in-law. They used the piece of cloth once, to wipe their feet, and then discarded it in the garbage!

The maid picked one up, made a blouse for herself, and then wore it to the king's palace when she visited a friend there. Well, the king found out what had happened, and promptly went with his entourage - all the king's men, and horses, and elephants - to meet Shali Bhadra.

Bhadra Shethani respectfully and warmly received King Shrenika and sent a word to Shali Bhadra that the king had arrived. In reply, Shali Bhadra asked Bhadra Shethani to buy whatever this 'king' was. Shethani explained to him that the king is the master, and is not a thing to buy.

Master!? Shali Bhadra thought that he himself was the master of everything. He was now disturbed. All this wealth, the palace, servants, and the beautiful wives who call him 'master', and now he has a master?

'Everyone does', the Shethani explained.

'Isn't there anyone who doesn't?'

'Only the Lord Mahavira. He does not have any master. He is the master of himself and shows others how to become like him', said Bhadra Shethani.

Shali Bhadra immediately came down, paid his respects to King Shrenika (who was also a devotee of Lord Mahavira), and declared his intention to give up everything and seek the shelter of Lord Mahavira and become his own master.

In this Katha, Shali Bhadra is the soul who is surrounded by illusion, and is unaware of his true form. The king represents the power of our Karmas –Punyas and Papas – which decides our fate, and acts like our master. Bhadra ('Benevolence') Shethani is the Guru or the teacher who shows us the truth, and points us in the right direction.

Sometimes, even a Guru cannot teach us. But then, experience is the best teacher, only if we are smart enough to learn from our mistakes. If we are capable of becoming Jinas, we are also capable of becoming our own Guru, as the next very interesting Katha illustrates.

ILACHI KUMARA

Ilachi Kumara was the son of a very rich Sheth (Kumara means 'a boy'). Why are all Kathas about the sons of the rich? Good question. All Kathas are about us and our Atma. The Atma is pure, bright and worth more than anything else. Therefore, we are rich, but we do not know our worth. Only a Guru can show us that. So, Ilachi was son of a rich man, and he fell in love with a poor tightrope walker's daughter, who had come to perform in his town.

Blinded by his love, he went to her father and expressed his wish to marry his daughter. The old man asked whether Ilachi knew any trade or craft. Of course, he didn't. He didn't have to. He was very rich. But the old man was very practical. He knew the real world in which the wealth comes and goes, and even major empires and civilizations could vanish.

The old man insisted that Ilachi Kumara will have to be able to earn his living from a craft, art, or any other vocation. Not wishing to be separated from his beloved woman, Ilachi decided to learn the art of tightrope walking and other highwire acts from her father.

Ilachi was a smart young man, and he didn't take very long to learn the skills. His girlfriend also helped him. Now all he had to do was perform in front of the king, please him, and get a good reward, then the young woman would be his. It was that easy.

The king was invited and the highwires were pulled between two tall buildings. Ilachi climbed up and started showing the unbelievably skillful acts. The king was watching. Ilachi's beloved woman was playing on the drum, and her father was calmly watching all this.

All the people were pleased and amazed. They knew that a big reward was due at any moment. The king was pleased too. But no reward came. The king's eyes were fixed on the beautiful and healthy outdoors woman playing on the drum, as if with her whole body.

He could sense that she was to marry Ilachi Kumara, once the show was over. The only way the king could get his desire fulfilled was to have Ilachi Kumara out of the way. If he did not give him the prize, Ilachi would get exhausted and would fall to his death.

Everybody was waiting impatiently for the reward to come, the woman was waiting to marry Ilachi Kumara, and the king was waiting to see Ilachi fall, so he himself could marry the woman. Meanwhile, Ilachi was trying to keep his balance, up there on a thin wire.

From there, he happened to see a Jain Sadhu in one of the rooms where a beautiful woman was offering many mouth-watering food items to him, but he was declining to accept any. This went on for some time and the monk left without taking anything.

Ilachi started wondering. 'Strange is the influence and power of our Karmas. They make us do all kinds of highwire acts and dangerous dances just to fulfil the demands of our spoiled monkey-like mind. Our desires make us slaves. These desires are not 'ours', we are 'theirs'.

That Sadhu was the master of his desires. He walked away from a beautiful woman's offerings. And look at me! I left my family, my friends, my riches, to learn a trade to please the king and to marry the woman of my desire. Now the king wishes me dead, so that he can marry her!' Right there on the highwire, Ilachi reached Kevala Gnyana.

We spend all our lives trying to achieve success at any cost, without ever wondering whether that success is worth the price, in terms of our family, our love, our principles, and our peace of mind. We end up trying to please the boss who knows that if (s)he praises our work, (s)he will have to give us a raise. Is all this really worth it? Or we can save our labors for better and higher pursuits?

There are hundreds of such interesting stories in Jain literature. They can save you from a lot of trouble and guide you along the right path. Request your teachers and parents to tell you a few more.

10. RECOMMENDED READING AND ACTIONS

Religion is a simple matter, so don't complicate it. Respect other religions. Do not try to convert anyone. Try to practice what you choose to. Do it in steps. Always take a vow.

Visit Derasaras, lecture-halls, etc. and stay there for a while at least, during the rituals.

Try to find your self, rather than losing your precious self in alcohol, drugs and tobacco smoke.

Learn Gujarati, Hindi (or whichever is your mother tongue), and/or Sanskrit. You will feel less like an outsider after you learn your mother tongue.

Meet other Jain youths, and organize lectures, camps, rituals, and festivals. When you go to India, or while you are in the United States or in the UK, visit various temples and other religious places.

Ask questions, even if you do not get satisfactory answers at first. Lack of answers shows you that even if you don't understand everything right away, you can still continue to practice.

Rituals and festivals are a fun way to start. Always try to find their significance.

Don't ever think that you know all there is to know about Jainism. Specifically, this book is only a drop from the great ocean.

Religion is a way to think and a way to live. It is not only a poem to read on a Sunday, or a fast once a year, or an occassional visit to a temple. You live it.

For further reading, look up 'Jainism' in various dictionaries and Encyclopedias. Don't miss Jain Art, Sculpture, Literature, etc. Inquire at the local public libraries and your school library, for books on Jainism.

Also read about non-violence, Gandhiji and Martin Luther King, Jr. Look up the literature on ecology and the environment.

Subscribe to or request a copy of the Jain newsletters published by the local Sangha, and other bodies. If there is nothing in it to interest you, let them know that.

Books can only tell you about the religion, but they are not **the** religion. Respect the books, but decide for yourself. Jainism is against violence of any kind, including that on one's mind.

May the Jinas bless you!

THE TREASURE CHEST

Jains use many greetings, slogans, symbols, Sutras and other writings. The first three are based on the Sutras. There are many other writings based on Sutras too. They include prayers praising the Lord. These are called Stuti, Stava, Stavan or Stotra, from Sanskrit Stu = to pray, to praise.*

Also included in Jain literature are writings which describe the virtues and vices, or do's and don'ts for us. These are to be read and thought over and then put into practice eventually. They are for self-study, and are called Sazzayas from Sanskrit word Svadhyaya (Sva = self, Adhyaya = study).

One can praise the idol and the temple and thereby pay respect. These songs are called Chaitya Vandana (Chaitya = a chapel, or a temple; Vandana= to bow). Some other writings are meant to worship the Lord with words and with holy objects, like a lamp, flowers, incense, water, etc. These songs are called Pujas (Puj = to worship). The act of offering the holy objects is also known as Puja.

Almost all of the classical writings are in poetry, making them easier to read and remember, and pleasant to recite. Some of these are pearls or gems and are filled with deep and beautiful meaning. We can only look at a small sample here.

I have given these below in Devanagri (Sanskrit/Hindi/Marathi) script, with their meaning in English. I have also given the pronunciation in English script. But I would urge you to use that only as a memory aid, and ask someone to read the original out loud for you to know the correct rhythm and pronunciation. English is not a phonetic language and many letters of the English alphabet can be pronounced in several ways. Take 'U' for example : But, Put, Busy, Bury, Laugh, etc. Therefore, even if I write everything in English, it would not help much.

On the other hand, let me assure you that it will be very easy for you to learn either Devanagri or Gujarati script (both are very similar). You can do that, just to get going, within only a day or two. Then you can read everything - yes, everything - yourself. This is not a commercial, but the publisher of this book has also published self-study books to learn these languages. You can learn either from those books or in many other ways, but do learn. That's your key to everything.

This point needs to be stressed more. Many Jain books are available in English, but they are meant either for the Indian intellectuals who are familiar with the Jain and Hindu traditions of thought and philosophy, or they are meant for non-Indian western readers familiar with Judeo-Christian tradition.

For obvious reasons, they are not quite suitable for you, and considering the limited resources and an enormous nature of the task, it will be far easier for you to learn a language than for someone to rewrite everything in English. Then, some day, maybe, you will want to rewrite Jain books in English poetry. Why not?

SYMBOLS

Symbols give a deep and elaborate message in a succint and visual manner. They are abstractions of a concept, and are meaningless in themselves if the message is forgotten. There are many symbols used by the Jains, but we will limit ourselves to just two.

SWASTIKA

The Swastika made infamous by the Nazis, is actually an ancient Aryan symbol, and it figures prominently in Hindu and Jain literature. The word 'Swastika' comes from Sanskrit 'Swasti', meaning 'May good come to you'.

The Swastika
is a benevolent symbol,
and implies no harm to anyone or anything

You will see the Swastika in the temples, Derasaras, in the Upashrayas, even in the houses, and as a part of many non-religious decorations and designs. The Nazi Swastika stands slanted at an angle, while the Jain - Hindu one rests horizontally on one of its sides.

It represents the cosmic cycle of birthts and rebirths, all connected at the center. One can go from one prong to the other via the center. The four prongs represent the four major kinds of life, viz. human race (Manushya), gods (Devas), the (plants and) animal life (Tiryanch), and those in the hell (Naraki). These are the four directions (Gatis) the Atma can take. It is not necessary to know which prong represents what. The symbol works as a whole.

The Swastika is a constant reminder to us to try to break out of the cycle of births and deaths and re-births, and to go above the Swastika, to the Siddha Shila, or the stonemarker of the Siddhas, the liberated souls. The Siddha Shila is represented by a crescent above the Swastika, and liberated soul is represented as a dot above Siddha Shila. The whole symbol looks like this:

The purpose of this life of ours is to free us from the cycle of births and to become a free Atma, a Siddha.

AUM

The symbol Aum (pronounced as Om) represents the same thing as the Swastika, with three prongs of the numeral '3' representing the heaven, the earth and the hell. The tail is the way out to the lands beyond. But the free soul goes out of this to sit above the Siddha Shila. There are several ways to write this symbol also. Aum as shown here is more often used by Hindus. Jains use this and several other versions of it.

SLOGANS

जय जिनेन्द्र ।

'Jay Jinendra'

'Victory be to the Lord Jinas'

'Jay Jinendra' is a salutation or a greeting. When Jains meet, they greet each other with their palms folded together and they say 'Jay Jinendra', meaning 'Victory be to the Lord Jinas'. The implication is that the Jinas are the real kings and victors. One can end a letter with 'Jay Jinendra from so and so'.

अहिंसा परमो धर्मः ।

'Ahinsa Paramo Dharmah'

Non-violence is the supreme religion.

The word Dharma means religion as well as duty. It is our highest duty to be non-violent. In English, you may see the word Ahinsa spelled as Ahimsa, and the latter is not quite correct.

पढमं नाणं तओ दया ।

'Padhamam Nanam Tao Daya'.

First knowledge, then Mercy.

Any mercy or pity shown without understanding the matter may do more harm than good. If a child is crying because a doctor is about to give him an injection, and a very merciful person 'saves' the child from the doctor, then that can hardly be called mercy.

मिच्छामि दुक्कडम् ।

'Michchhami Dukkadam'.

'May my misdeed be null and void'

'I apologize for my wrongs' is the most famous slogan of atonoment used by the Jains. It is used in writing letters, or cards, or in person, and during the Pratikamanas. One apologizes for one's wrong-doings, with the determination and promise of not repeating the same misdeed.

परस्परोपग्रहो जीवानाम् ।
'Parasparopagraho Jivanam'.

'The life forms are under obligation to one another.'

Life depends on other life, therefore it is our supreme duty not to destroy other life, especially unnecessarily (Paraspara = mutual, Upagraho = obligation, Jivanam = of the life forms).

सम्यग् ज्ञान दर्शन चारित्राभ्याम् मोक्षः ।
'Samyag Gnana Darshan Charitrabhyam Mokshah'.

It is only through the right knowledge, the right wisdom and the right action that the liberation is achieved.

These are not three different ways, but only one way, in which all three are required. Even if only one of these is missing, that would not do.

सवि जीव करुं शासनरसी ।
'Savi Jiva Karun Shasan Rasi.'

Let me get others interested in Jinas' word.

This is in Gujarati and in Hindi. It expresses the joy of being Jain and a desire to spread the word of the Jinas to everybody. Literally it says, may I make (Karun), all (Savi) living things (Jiva), interested (Rasi) in the realm (Shasan) of the Jinas.

GEMS FROM THE SUTRAS

Now let us look at samples from a few Sutras. There is no reason why you cannot memorize these if you so want to. As children, we had memorized book full of Sutras without understanding them at first. We did learn the meanings later. It is fun either way.

One friendly warning. In Sanskrit, many successive words are joined together. Therefore the writing may look more complicated than what it really is. Do not let the long-looking words bother you. I have broken down such compound words into their component parts, whenever it is possible.

खामेमि सव्वजीवे   Khamemi savva jive

सव्वे जीवा खमन्तु मे ।   Savve jiva khamantu me

मित्ति मे सव्व भूएसु   Mitti me savva bhuesu

वेरं मज्झं न केणई ॥   Veram mazzam na kena i.

-from the **Vandittu Sutra**

'I forgive all the living beings. I urge them to forgive me. I have amity for all beings, but enmity towards none.'

This is the spirit one wishes to be in all the times, but especially when one is about to leave or to die. It is not easy to think of this at the end, unless one has thought of it repeatedly during the life. This is one of the most famous stanzas, and it embodies the principle of universal atonement or Michchhami Dukkadam.

दर्शनं देवदेवस्य   Darshanam deva-devasya

दर्शनं पापनाशनम् ।   Darshanam papa-nashanam

दर्शनं स्वर्गसोपानम्   Darshanam svarga-sopanam

दर्शनं मोक्षसाधनम् ॥   Darshanam moksha-sadhanam.

'The sight of the idol of the Lord, the God of all gods, is destroyer of all sins. It is a step toward the heavens, and is a means to the liberation of the soul.'

You may recite the above prayer either in your mind or aloud without disturbing someone else, with folded hands, in front of an idol.

144

तुभ्यं नमस्त्रिभुवनार्तिहराय नाथ !
तुभ्यं नमः क्षितितलामलभूषणाय !
तुभ्यं नमस्त्रिजगतः परमेश्वराय !
तुभ्यं नमो जिन ! भवोदधिशोषणाय !

Tubhyam namastri-bhuvanarti-haraya Natha !
Tubhyam namah kshiti-talamala-bhushanaya !
Tubhyam namastri-jagatah Parameshvaraya !
Tubhyam namo Jina ! Bhavodadhi-shoshanaya !

- from the **Bhaktamara Stotra** by
Shri Mantung Suri

'I bow to you O Master !
The remover of all aflictions from the heaven, the earth and the hell
        (the three worlds).
I bow to you, O The adoration of the face of this earth !
I bow to you, O the supreme Lord of the three worlds !
I bow to you, O Jina, who can make the great ocean called Sansara disppear !'

(You may recite the above prayer also, in front of an idol.)

स्त्रीणां शतानिशतशो जनयन्ति पुत्रान्
नान्यासुतं त्वदुपमं जननी प्रसूता ।
सर्वादिशो दधति भानि सहस्ररश्मिं
प्राच्येव दिग्जनयति स्फुरदंशुजालम् ॥

Strinam shatani shatasho janayanti putran
Nanya sutam tvadupamam janani prasuta
Sarva disho dadhati bhani sahastra-rashmim
Prachyev-dig janayati sfurdanshujalam.

- from the **Bhaktamara Stotra**

(O Jina!) Hundreds and hundreds of women deliver babies everyday, (but) no one gives birth to the one like you. All the parts of the sky can carry small lights but only the East can give rise to the Sun.

सोऽहं तथापि तव भक्तिवशान्मुनीश !
कर्तुं स्तवं विगतशक्तिरपि प्रवृत्तः ।
प्रित्यात्मवीर्यमविचार्य मृगो मृगेन्द्रम्
नाभ्येति किं निज शिशोः परिपालनार्थम् ?

Soham tathapi tava bhaktivashan, Muneesh !
Kartum stavam vigatashaktirapi pravruttah
Prityatmaviryam-avicharya mrugo mrugendram
Nabhyeti kim nija-shisho-paripalanartham ?

- from the **Bhaktamara Stotra**

Even though I am like that (incapable, foolish, and weak), I am embarking upon composing this song to praise you, only out of love and devotioin for you. Doesn't a doe (a female deer), out of love for her young ones, without any regard for her own weakness, confront a lion?

त्वं तारको जिन ! कथं भविनांतमेव ?
त्वामुद्वहन्ति हृदयेन यदुत्तरन्तः ।
यद्वाद्रुतिस्तरति यज्जलमेष नूनम्
अन्तर्गतस्य मरुतः स किलानुभावः ॥

Tvum tarako, Jina ! Katham bhavinantameva?
Tvamudvahanti hrudayen yaduttarantah
Yadva-druti-starati-yaj-jalam-esh noonam-
Antargatasya marutah sa kilanubhavah !

- from the **Kalyana Mandira Stotra** by
Shri Siddhasena Divakara Suri

How come you are called 'the savior', even though with you sitting in their heart, people go across the ocean of the Sansara (that is, they actually save you)? Indeed, it is the air in the floating tube (in the original, it is a leather water bag, called a Mashak, which you have probably never seen) that makes it float (that is, you are indeed, the savior)!

The Bhaktamara and the Kalyana Mandira Stotras are so beautiful and lyrical, that you may want to memorize them, and a poet among you may like to translate these into English. Bhaktamara was written by Shri Manatunga Suri and the Kalyana Mandira was written by Shri Siddhasena Divakara Suri. We read their stories earlier.

कमठे धरणेन्द्रे च
स्वोचितं कर्म कुर्वति ।
प्रभुस्तुल्य मनोवृत्तिः
पार्श्वनाथः श्रियेस्तु वः ॥

Kamathe-Daranendre cha
Svochitam karma kurvati
Prabhustulya manovruttihi
Parshwanathah Shriyestu vah!

- from **Sakalarhat Sutra**
by **Shri Hemachandra Suri**

With Kamatha the rain-god, and Dharanendra the king of Snakes doing whatever they see fit (the former trying to drown Lord Parshwa Natha, and the latter trying to keep him afloat), the Lord feels the equanimity towards both of them. May such Lord Parshwa Natha bless you.

कृतापराधे ऽपि जने
कृपामंथरतारयोः ।
ईषदबास्पार्द्रयोर्भद्रं
श्रीवीरजिननेत्रयोः ॥

Krutaparadhe-pi-jane
Krupamanthartarayo
Ishad-bashp-ardrayor-bhadram
Shri Vira Jin-netrayoh.

- from the **Saklarhat Stotra**

'Even to those who are guilty of troubling Him, the Lord Mahavira's eyes are moist and warm, full of benevolence for them too.'

Sakalarhat (Sakala = all, Arhat = Arihanta) is the Stavana of all twenty-four Jinas.

श्री श्रमणसंघस्य शांतिर्भवतु !
श्री पौरजनस्य शांतिर्भवतु !
श्री पौरमुख्याणाम् शांतिर्भवतु !
श्री गोष्ठीकानाम् शांतिर्भवतु !
श्री ब्रह्मलोकस्य शांतिर्भवतु !

Shri shramana Sanghasya shantir-bhavatu !
Shri paur-janasya shantir-bhavatu !
Shri paur-mukhyanam shantir-bhavatu !
Shri goshthikanam shantir-bhavatu !
Shri brahma-lokasya shantir-bhavatu !

- from The **Great Peace Song**

May peace be to the whole Sangha, may peace be to all the town-people, may peace be to all the town-leaders, may peace be to all the religious assemblies, may peace be to the whole universe. (These lines are chosen out of sequence).

***   ***   ***   ***   ***   ***

उपसर्गाः क्षयं यान्ति
छिद्यन्ते विघ्नवल्यः ।
मनः प्रसन्नतामेति
पूज्यमाने जिनेश्वरे ॥

Upasargaha kshayum yanti
Chhidyante vighnavallaya
Manah prasannatameti
Poojyamane Jineshvare.

सर्वमंगलमांगल्यं
सर्व कल्याणकारणम् ।
प्रधानं सर्व धर्माणां
जैनं जयति शासनम् ॥

Sarva mangala mangalyam
Sarva kalyana-karanam
Pradhanam sarva dharmanam
Jainam jayati shasanam.

- from the **Great Piece Song**, and also from the **Uvasaggaharum Sutra** by Shri Bhadra Bahu Swami

'All the troubles disintegrate, the shackles of obstacles break, the mind achieves a pleasant state, wherever and whenever the Lord Jinas are worshipped.

The holiest of all holy things, the cause of all the benevolence, the greatest of all religions, the Jainism reigns supreme.'

[Note that the second stanza above is not meant to be a put down for other religions. If you have read this book thus far, you are not going to misunderstand this now. The word 'religions' is a poor translation for the word Dharma, which means duty, among many other things. 'Reigns supreme' has more to do with Jainism's victory over sins, rather than over other religions for whom Jainism advocates nothing but understanding and tolerance and respect.]

देवदाण विंद चंद सुर वंद हट्ठ तुट्ठ जिट्ठ परम
लट्ठ रुव धंत रुप्प पट्ट से य सुध्ध निध्ध धवल ।
दंत पंति संति सत्ति किित्ति मुत्ति जुत्ति गुत्ति पवर
दित्त ते अ वंद धेअ सव्व लोअ भावि अप्प भावणे अ पईस मे समाहिं ॥   (नारायओ)

Deva-dana-vinda-chanda-sura-vanda-hattha-tuttha-jittha-parama
Lattha-ruva-dhanta-ruppa-patta-se-a-suddha-niddha-dhavala
Danta-panti-santi-satti-kitti-mutti-jutti-gutti-pavara
Ditta-te a-vanda-dhe a-savva-lo a-bhavi appa-bhava-ne a-pa i-sa me- sama him.

(Naraya-o)

-from **Shri Ajit Shanti Stava**

Ask someone to recite the above to you just for the lovely rhythm of it. The stanza is from one of the Nine Memorables — Shri Ajita Shanti Stava, which is a prayer of Shri Ajita Natha and Shri Shanti Natha (the second and the sixteenth Tirthankaras, respectively). The Ajita Shanti Stava is a museum of many kinds of meters of Ardha Magadhi poetry. The above stanza is in the meter 'Naraya-o'.

SUTRAS

THE NAVAKAR MANTRA

नमो अरिहंताणं

Namo Arihantanam

नमो सिद्धाणं

Namo Sidhdhanam

नमो आयरिआणं

Namo Ayarianam

नमो उवज्झायाणं

Namo Uvajzayanam

नमो लोए सव्व साहूणं ।

Namo lo-e savva Sahunam

एसो पंच नमुक्कारो

Eso pancha namukkaro

सव्वपावप्पणासणो ।

Savva pavappanasano

मंगलाणं च सव्वेसिं

Mangalanam cha savvesim

पढमं हवई मंगलम् ॥

Padhamam havai mangalam.

149

'I bow to the Arihantas. I bow to the Siddhas. I bow to the Acharyas. I bow to the Upaddhyayas. I bow to all the Sadhus in this world.'

'Bowing to these five (aspired beings) 'is destroyer of all sins. And of all the holy things, the first (and the holiest) it is.'

This is the most important prayer. We have talked about it earlier in the Part I. You should know this prayer by heart. To be able to say it out loud is the minimum evidence that you are a Jain.

SANSAR-DAVANAL-DAH SUTRA.

by Shri Hari Bhadra Suri.

This is for you to read or listen to someone else read it to you. To a beginner, the Sanskrit writings are generally difficult to read, because of many conjoined consonants, and because of the practice of joining the adjacent words together, without any hyphens. It takes a little acquaintance to enjoy that marvelous language.

For a Sanskrit poet, it is a singular achievement to compose a poem without any conjoined consonants (called जोडाक्षर, or 'joined letters'). The following Sutra by Shri Hari Bhadra Suri is an example of such a poem. He died before composing the last three lines, which were then completed by the Sangha. We did go over his story.

संसारदावानलदाहनीरं
संमोहधूलीहरणे समीरं ।
मायारसादारणसारसीरं
नमामि वीरं गिरिसारधीरं ॥

भावावनामसुरदानवमानवेन
चूलाविलोलकमलावलिमानितानि ।
संपूरिताभिनत लोक समीहितानि
पामंनमामि जिनराज ! पदानि तानि ॥

150

बोधागाधं सुपदपदवीनीरपूराभिरामं
जीवाहिंसाविरललहरी संगमाऽगाहदेहम् ।
चूलावेलं गुरुगममणि संकुलं दूरपारं
सारं वीराऽगमजलनिधिं सादरं साधु सेवे ॥

आमूलाऽलोलधूली बहुलपरिमला लीढलोलालिमाला
झंकारारावसारा ! मलदलकमलागारभूमिनिवासे !
छायासंभारसारे ! वरकमलकरे ! तारहाराभिरामे !
वाणीसंदोहदेहे ! भवविरहवरं देहि मे देवि ! सारम् ॥

Sansara-davanala-daha-neeram
Sam-moh-dhuli-harane-samiram
Maya-rasadaranasarasiram
Namami Viram ! Girisaradhiram. 1.

Bhavavanam-asur-danava-manavena
Chula-vilola-kamalavali-malitani
Sumpurita-bhinata-lokasami-hitani
Pamam-namami Jinaraja !   Padani-tani. 2.

Bodhagadham-supada-padavi-nira-pura-bhiramam
Jiva-hinsa-virala-lahari-sangam-agaha-deham
Chulavelam-gurugamamani-sunkulam-duraparam
Saram-vira-gamajalanidhim-sadaram sadhu seve. 3.

Aamool-alola-dhuli-bahula-parimala lidha-lolali-mala
Jhankara-ravasara-maladala-kamala-gara-bhumi-nivase
Chhaya-sambhara-sare-vara-kamala-kare-tara-hara-bhirame
Vani-sandohadehe bhava-vira-havaram dehi me Devi ! Saram. 4.

Note that in the first line of the fourth stanza, the 'L' sound occurs eleven times. In English, this is called Alliteration. We will not go into the meaning of this Sutra, because it is easily available in many text books.

ABOUT THE ATICHARA SUTRA

At least once a year, Jains go over this check-list of transgressions, and apologize in their own minds, in front of a Guru (a monk). There is no confession of any sin here, but you are made aware of it, and the expectation is that you will not repeat the sinful behavior.

Sutra ('a thread') is a religious writing which ties the points together. The ancients used to write several Sutras on palm leaves, collect them together with a knot. Such book was called a Grantha (= 'a knot). Any scholarly volume is called a Grantha.

The 'Atichara Sutra' lists many Aticharas (transgressions). The original is in old Gujarati. It is one of the few Sutras which are in Gujarati rather than in Sanskrit or in Ardha-Magadhi, which are the grandmother and the mother of Gujarati.

We will look at only some parts of the Sutra, and that also in a loose and sketchy translation. Your parents may be able to read to you the original full version if you request them to. Don't be surprised if they themselves have trouble with it since the language is old, and archaic. Many of the things, creatures and actions mentioned therein are no longer parts of our daily lives today. But you will find it very interesting.

So, take a break for a few minutes, then sit upright in a quiet, well-lit place and read slowly. Maybe you will find yourself in violation of several Acharas (code of behavior), but don't despair. Wake up and start counting again. That's the idea.

THE ATICHARA SUTRA

The proper conduct (Achara) in relation to knowledge (Gnyana), understanding (Darshana), and behavior (Charitra), is required. Proper practice requires proper training (Tapa) and proper perfomance (Virya).

In my conduct relating to these five pursuits, *any deviation or transgression that may have taken place during the last year (or four months, or the fortnight), grossly or minutely, knowingly or unknowingly, I seek forgivance for that with my mind, my speech and my body.*

A. Conduct Relating to Knowledge:

1. Did not study at proper time.
2. Studied without proper respect or care
3. Did not recite the Sutras correctly. Garbled up their narration, did not tell the meaning clearly. Forgot the Sutras.
4. Touched with feet, or accidently kicked books or religious equipments, saliva fell on the books, used books as pillows.
5. Ate or drank while reading.
6. Did not understand, or showed indifference to the knowkedge.
7. Did not take care even though capable to do so.
8. Despised the knowledgeable ones, disturbed others in their studies, displayed pride of our knowledge, laughed at someone's stuttering.
9. Misrepresented the scriptures.

In my conduct relating to knowledge, *any deviation .... and my body.*

B. Conduct Relating to Understanding:

1. Had doubts about the Lord, the Guru, and the religion. Had doubts about the value of practicing the religion.
2. On seeing the 'success' of people with bad conduct, developed a dislike for the good one.
3. Did not appreciate the virtuous ones in the Sangha. Did not stop them from a lapse in conduct.
4. Misappropriated the money meant for the temple, or charity.
5. Quarrelled with another Jain.
6. Did not respect the idol. Passed urine or cleaned nose on the temple grounds. Eating, playing, joking around, etc. were done there. Did not respect the Guru.

In my conduct relating to Understanding *any deviation...and my body.*

C. Conduct Relating to Behavior:

1. Became careless in moving around, or in speaking.
2. Harbored bad thoughts, of hunting or killing.
3. Had doubts about faith in Arihanta, and worshipped various gods and other elements, idols, or temples for tangible gain in this or the next birth. Got confused and enticed by other monks and their apparent miracles. Learned improper and the so-called scriptures. Kept vows and Vratas of all kinds for some gains.
4. Under this section - behavior - are included the twelve Vratas of Shravakas:

Transgressions Regarding These Vratas

1. The Vrata of Gross Non-Violence.

Treated servants with cruelty. Tied animals very tightly, inflicted deep wounds on them, sterilized them or pierced their nose, ear, etc. Did not feed them on time, ate before feeding them, put them in a lock up, got them killed. In our food and fire-wood, carelessly killed or destroyed bugs, animals or their nests, in moving things around crushed or mutilated creatures, did not keep Jayana.

In my conduct relating to Non-Violence, *any deviation...and my body.*

2. The Vrata of Truth.

Lied, revealed someone's secrets, embezzled the entrusted money, deceived others about land, money, animals, or in social relations. Used curses, and hurtful speech.

In my conduct relating to Truth, *any deviation...and my body.*

3. The Vrata of Non-Stealing.

Took someone's things without those being given, received stolen goods, conspired with thieves, gave them lunch, acted against the law, mixed new/old, good/bad etc. to deceive. Used defective weight scales, took or gave bribe, breached trust, tucked away money secretly.

In my conduct relating to Non-Stealing, *any deviation...and my body.*

4. The Vrata of Celibacy.

Instead of remaining content with one's wife and avoiding other women, had relations with the women in one's custody, or with a widow, prostitute, someone else's wife. Had sweet talks with other such women. Arranged marriages or divorces, lusted in mind, stared at women's bodies, had intense sexual desire, had transgressions in dreams. (Although not explicitly stated, the above applies to both the sexes.)

In my conduct relating to Celibacy, *any deviation...and my body.*

5. The Vrata of Non-Hoarding.

Hoarded grain, wealth, land, real estate, silver, gold, other metal, servants, animals, etc., any of these nine items. Hoarded them for relatives,

In my conduct relating to Non-Hoarding, *any deviation...and my body.*

The Sixth through Twelfth Vratas.

Ate any of the 22 uneatables namely potatoes, onions, garlic, 32 multiple life-forms including root vegetable (ginger, raddish, carrots), unknown fruits.
Kept pets.
Made big beginnings.
Gambled, put a curse on someone, conducted or watched animal fights.
Did not take good care of the monks; even though capable, did not take care of other Jains, or temples, or charities.
Did not give to the poor and to the weak.
In good days wished to live longer, and in bad ones wished to die.

In my conduct relating to the sixth through twelfth Vratas, *any deviation.....and my body.*

D. Conduct of Tapa:

Did not do the external (physical) Tapas properly, did not keep the Pachchakhana, took unboiled water, vomitted during Tapa.

In the internal Tapas, did not maintain humility and decency towards the Lord, Guru, and the Sangha. Did not help the younger, the older, the ones in Tapa. Did not do self-studies by reading, asking, revising, etc.

In my conduct relating to Tapa, *any deviation...and my body.*

E. Conduct of Virya:

In reading, or in helping others or in Tapas, or in religious act and rituals, became lazy, did not follow the Vidhi properly, sat through absent-mindedly, or went through the Vidhi hurriedly.

In my conduct relating to Virya, *any deviation...and my body.*

Preached against the scriptures, or misrepresented them. Commited any of the eighteen abodes of sin. Against Jina's words, either did anything, or got it done, or encouraged someone else to do it.

In this fashion, in my conduct relating to the duties of Shravaks including the twelve Vratas, there are one hundred and twenty four Aticharas (we did not list all of them).

In my conduct relating to these, *any deviation or transgression that may have taken place during the last year (or four months, or the fortnight), grossly or minutely, knowingly or unknowingly, I seek forgivance for that with my mind, my speech and my body.*

* *

What I have given here in the Treasure Chest are not necessarily the best, or the most representative examples. There are many more Sutras, and the deeper you go in, the more you will enjoy and appreciate them.

What we have done in this part of the book is to have a glimpse of what Jainism is all about. This is neither a guide, nor an Encyclopedia, nor an instruction manual. Many such books are available. Jainism is your religion, and its future, like that of your own, is in your hands.

Jay Jinendra!

END OF

THE TREASURE CHEST

GLOSSARY

This Glossary lists all the technical and foreign language terms used in this book. Items appearing in the Treasure Chest are excluded. Almost all the terms are in Sanskrit, or in Ardha-Magadhi. A few are in Gujarati (Guj). Although the English spellings shown here are phonetic, they are a poor guide for pronunciation, and they provide only an approximation. The serious students are advised to learn the correct pronunciations from someone who knows, or can read those given in the Devanagari script below.

'A' is pronounced as the first 'A' in AMERICA, while the underlined '<u>A</u>' is pronounced as the last 'A' in AMERIC<u>A</u>. Note that almost all terminal 'A's - e.g., in Rama, Mahavira, Raga, Prasanna, etc. - are pronounced as A, and not as <u>A</u>. In some feminine names, as in Chandan<u>a</u>, Bhadr<u>a</u>, etc. the terminal 'a' is pronunced as the last 'a' in Americ<u>a</u>. Only the main entries are thus marked.

The entries are arranged in the English alphabetical order. The main entry is followed by the same in the Devanagari script (used for Sanskrit, Hindi and Marathi languages). Then the description is given. The words in Italics appear as separate entries in this Glossary. For locating any of these entries in the book, please refer to the Index.

Abhaya Kum<u>a</u>ra	अभय कुमार	Son of king Shrenik
Abhigraha	अभिग्रह	A special vow to end a *Tapa* only when certain conditions are met.
<u>A</u>bu	आबु	A mountain in Rajasthan, on which the exquisitely carved *Delwada* temples are situated
Mt.-	माउन्ट-	Same as above
A<u>cha</u>ra	आचार	Code of conduct, proper conduct
A<u>cha</u>rya	आचार्य	The head monk, who delivers sermons
<u>A</u>dishvara	आदीश्वर	The first *Tirthankara* of the present *Chauvisi*
<u>A</u>gama	आगम	Jain scriptures. There are 45 *Agamas*.
Ahins<u>a</u>	अहिंसा	Non-violence, the first of the five *Vratas*
Ajita	अजित	Un-conquered (A = un, Ji = to win)
-Natha	-नाथ	the second *Tirthankara*
An<u>a</u>cha<u>ra</u>	अनाचार	lack of *Achara*
Anumodana	अनुमोदन	Encouragement, cheering along

157

Arati	आरति	worshipping with a lamp
Ardha Magadhi	अर्धमागधी	the language of Jain scriptures (Ardha = half, and Magadhi = from the State of Magadha, today's Bihar, in Eastern India)
Arihanta	अरिहंत	One who conquered oneself, attained the *Kevala Gnyana*, and was still alive (Ari = enemies, Hant = are killed)
Atichara	अतिचार	transgressions in practice of *Achar*
Atma	आत्मा	soul (= self)
Aum	ओम्	a symbol (see the Treasure Chest)
Avashyaka	आवश्यक	parts of a *Pratikramana*. There are six such parts in a *Pratikramana*. Avashyaka = essential
Ayambila	आयंबिल	an *Ekasanun* in which all seasoning and spices are avoided.
Babu	बाबु	mister, Mr. (In *Bengali*)
Bahubaliji	बाहुबलीजी	Lord *Rushabha Deva*'s son. (Bahu = upper arm, bala = strength)
Bamano	बामणो	(Guj.) a curse meaning 'a Brahmin', a beggar
Bengali	बेंगाली	a person from the State of Bengal in North Eastern India. Calcutta is in West Bengal. a language derived from *Sanskrit*.
Besanun	बेसणुं	(Guj.) partial fasting in which only two meals are taken during a day
Bhadra	भद्रा	*Shali Bhadra*'s mother (Bhadra = bene-volence)
Bhamato	भामटो	(Guj.) a curse meaning, a 'Brahmin', a beggar
Bihar	बिहार	a State in Eastern India, near Calcutta (Vihar = a *Budhdhist* monastery)
Brahma	ब्रह्मा	the Hindu god of creation, father of *Sarasvati*
Brahman	ब्राह्मण	a Brahmin. A tradition of Indian philosophy, based on appeasing various gods to achieve worldly gains, as opposed to the *Shraman* tradition from which *Jainism* came about
Buddha	बुदध	Lord Buddha, the enlightened one (Budh = to learn)
Buddhu	बुदधु	(Guj.) a curse meaning, a Buddhist. Innocent.

158

Chaitya	चैत्य	a chapel, a temple, *Derasar, Jinalaya*
-Paripati	-परिपाटी	visiting all the temples in the town, especially after the *Paryushana*
-Vandana	-वंदन	a ritual of paying respect to the temple and the idol of the Lord
Chandana Bala	चंदन बाला	the enslaved princess who offered food to Lord *Mahavira*, and became the first *Sadhvi*. (Chandana = sandlewood, bala = a girl)
Chandra	चंद्र	the Moon
-Prabhu	-प्रभु	the seventh *Tirthankara*
Chaumasi	चौमासी	pertaining to 'four months' (Chau = four, mas = months)
-Pratikramana	-प्रतिक्रमण	the *Pratikramana* that is done three times a year
Chauvihara	चौविहार	not eating any of the four kinds of food after the sundown (Chau = four, Ahar = food))
Chauvisattho	चौविसत्थो	prayer of 24 *Tirthankaras*, (Chau = four, Visa = twenty)
Chauvisi	चोवीसी	(Guj.) twenty- four-some, 24 Tirthankaras
Dhyana	ध्यान	meditation
Delawada	देलवाडा	a town on Mount Abu where famous Jain temples are situated
Derasara	देरासर	a Jain temple
Deva	देव	a god, the 'shining one'
Rushabha-	ऋषभ-	the first *Tirthankara, Adishvara*
Devanagari	देवनागरी	a script (see the middle column) used for *Hindi, Marathi,* and *Sanskrit*
Devasi	देवसि	the evening *Pratikramana* (Divas = a day)
Devi	देवी	a goddess
Dharanendra	धरणेन्द्र	the king of snakes who lifted up Lord *Parshva Natha,* when *Kamatha* tried to drown him
Dharma	धर्म	religion, duty
-Natha	-नाथ	the fifteenth *Tirthankara*

Digambara	दिगंबर	a sect of Jainism, in which the *Sadhus* do not wear any clothes (Dig = East and other directions, Ambar = clothing; literally, 'sky-clad')
Diksha	दीक्षा	initiation into monkhood
Divo	दीवो	(Guj.) a lamp
Mangal-	मंगल-	a holy lamp
Diwali	दिवाली	(Guj.) the Festival of Lights, the last day of the Hindu year of King Vikrama, the day Lord *Mahavira* achieved *Moksha* (died)
Dvesha	द्वेष	a dislike for someone, to dispise
Dwadashangi	द्वादशांगी	a collection of twelve original Jain scriptures, compiled by *Gautam Swami* and other *Ganadharas* of Lord *Mahavira*
Ekasanun	एकासणुं	a partial fast, wherein only one meal is taken in a day
Gabharo	गभारो	(Guj.) an inner sanctum of a temple, in which the idol or *Murti* is kept
Ganadhara	गणधर	the chief disciples of a *Tirthankara*
Ghadi	घडी	twenty four minutes. A *Samayika* lasts for two Ghadis.
Garbhadvara	गर्भद्वार	a *Gabharo*, the inner sanctum of a temple, in which the *Murti* or the idol is kept.
Gautama	गौतम	Lord *Buddha*'s first name. Also, *Gautama Swami* who was the first *Ganadhara* of Lord *Mahavira*.
Gnyana	ज्ञान	knowledge
Avadhi-	अवधि-	- of what is going on in the world
Kevala-	केवल-	- pure and ultimate
Manah-Paryava-	मनहःपर्यव-	- of thoughts of the other person
Mati-	मति-	- born of inherent sense
Shruta-	श्रुत-	- inborn and acquired from the scriptures
Gomateshwaraji	गोमतेश्वरजी	a 60 feet tall statue of *Bahubaliji* at *Shravan Belagoda*

Gujarata	गुजरात	a State in Western India, north of Bombay
Gujarati	गुजराती	people of *Gujarata*, their language derived from *Sanskrit*
Hem	हेम	gold
-Chandra	-चंद्र	- moon. Hemchandracharya was a great monk known for his extensive writings of the scriptures, grammar, etc.
Hindi	हिंदी	a language derived from *Sanskrit*, it is the National Language of India.
Hindu	हिंदु	an Indian, or a follower of Hinduism
Indra	ईन्द्र	king of gods. Indra is a title, not a name.
Dharanendra	धरणेन्द्र	king of snake gods, who kept *Parshwa Natha* afloat
Indrani	ईन्द्राणी	Queen of gods, a title, 'wife of Indra'
Ishvara	ईश्वर	God, *Prabhu*, *Bhagawana*
Adi-	अदि-	the first *Tirthankara*
Gomateshwara	गोमतेश्वर	a statue of *Bahubaliji* at *Shravan (Shraman) Belagoda*
Jain	जैन	a follower of *Jinas*
Jayanti	जयंती	a birthday
Mahavira-	महावीर-	- of Lord *Mahavira*
Jina	जिन	one who has conquered oneself (Ji = to win)
Jinalaya	जिनालय	a temple of *Jina*, Jain temple (Alaya = abode)
Jodakshara	जोडाक्षर	(Guj.) a conjoined consonant
Joga	जोग	an union *(Yog)* of stars, of circumstances; of mind, speech and action.
Vartaman-	वर्तमान-	prevalent-. 'Circumstances permitting'
Kalaha	कलह	a quarrel, one of the 18 *Papa Sthanakas*
Kalpa Sutra	कल्प सूत्र	a holy book, written by *Bhadra Bahu Swami*, describing the life of Lord *Mahavira* and his disciples

Kama	काम	desire, one of the 18 *Papa Sthanakas*
Kamatha	कमठ	the rain god who tried to drown Lord *Parshwa Natha*
Karana	करण	doing something
Karavana	करावण	getting something done by others
Kausagga	काउसग्ग	see *Kayotsarga*
Kaushika	कौशिक	the angry monk, better known as Chanda (angry) Kaushika, who became a ferocious snake of the same name
Kayotsarga	कायोत्सर्ग	to 'count' or recite *Navakara Mantra* several times, to remind us that we are the *Atma*, and not a mere body.
Krodha	क्रोध	anger, one of the 18 *Papa Sthanakas*
Kshatriya	क्षत्रिय	a Caste of warriors, one of the four Castes. Jainism does not believe in the Caste system
Kshira	क्षीर	milk
-Samudra	-समुद्र	-sea, the Milk Sea whose water is used to bathe the newborn Lord, on top of *Mt. Meru.*
Lanchhana	लांछन	'a blemish', a sign identifying an idol, e.g., a lion indicates the idol of Lord *Mahavira*
Laxmi	लक्ष्मी	the Hindu goddess of wealth, wife of Lord Vishnu
Lobha	लोभ	averice, greed. One of the 18 *Papa Sthanakas*
Luccho	लुच्चो	(Guj.) a curse meaning, 'cunning' ('Jain', from *Lunchan*)
Lunchana	लुंचन	pulling off their hairs by Jain monks
Magadha	मगध	a State in ancient India, today's *Bihar*
Magadhi	मागधी	a language used in Magadha
Ardha-	अर्ध-	a language of Magadha, in which most Jain scriptures are written. It is daughter of Sanskrit, and mother of Gujarati and other languages.
Mahabharata	महाभारत	an Indian epic, which incorporates the Hindu

		holy book Bhagavad Gita
Maharashtra	महाराष्ट्र	a State in Western India, with Bombay as one of the major cities
Mahavira	महावीर	the 24th *Tirthankara,* and 'founder' of Jainism as it is practiced today
-Jayanti	-जयंती	birthday of Lord *Mahavira,* the 13th day of the bright fortnight of the Hindu calendar month Chaitra
Malli Natha	मल्लि नाथ	the only *Tirthankara* who was a woman, the 19th *Tirthankara*
Mangala	मंगल	holy
Divo	-दीवो	-(Guj.) lamp, the Holy Lamp used in the nightly ritual to close the temple
Mantra	मंत्र	a group of words given by a Guru, to be recited repeatedly
Navakara-	नवकार-	a *Mantra* starting with 'Namo Arihantanun'
Marathi	मराठी	a North Indian language, in Bombay. Marathi is derived from *Sanskrit,* and both these languages use the same *Devanagaɪ* script (see the middle column)
Maya	माया	infatuation, one of the 18 *Papa Sthanakas Illusion* in Hindu scriptures
Meru	मेरु	a holy mountain, possibly the Himalayas
Moti	मोती	a pearl
-Shah Sheth	-शाह शेठ	- (Guj.) a *Sheth,* who built several temples in Bombay, *Palitana,* etc.
Moksha	मोक्ष	salvation, Nirvana
Mount	माउन्ट	a mountain
-Abu	-आबु	where there are many beautiful temples
-Meru	-मेरु	the Himalayas, where the newborn Lord is taken and bathed in the water from the *Kshira Samudra*
Muhurta	मुहूर्त	the duration of a *Samayika,* two *Ghadis,* or 48 minutes. There are several other and more common meanings of this word, but they are not relevent here
Murti	मूर्ति	an idol
-Puja	-पूजा	-worship

163

Natha	नाथ	a master
Ajita-	अजित-	the 2nd *Tirthankara*
Dharma-	धर्म-	the 15th *Tirthankara*
Malli-	मल्लि--	the 19th *Tirthankara,* who was a woman
Shanti-	शान्ति-	the 16th *Tirthankara*
Navakara	नवकार	a *Sutra* starting with 'Namo Arihantanun'
-Mantra	-मंत्र	same as *Navakara*
Pali	पाली	a language of the ancient State of *Magadha,* used in the *Buddhist* scriptures. It is a daughter of *Sanskrit,* like *Ardha-Magadhi*
Papa	पाप	a sin
-Sthanaka	-स्थानक	- abode of sins, there are 18
Paramatma	परमात्मा	the liberated soul, *Siddha.* In Hindu tradition, God.
Parva	पर्व	a festival
Paryushana	पर्युषण	a *Jain* festival of eight holy days
Prabhu	प्रभु	a master, *Natha, Ishvara, Swami*
Chandra-	चंद्र-	- the Moon. The 8th *Tirthankara*
Padma-	पद्म-	- a lotus. The 6th *Tirthankara*
Prasada	प्रसाद	a blessing, the food that has been offerred to the Hindu gods, which is then consumed
Pratikramana	प्रतिक्रमण	a ritual of extended or modified *Samayika,* to do atonement
Chaumasi-	चौमासी-	a *Pratikramana* done three times a year
Devasi-	देवसि-	the evening one
Pakshik-	पाक्षिक-	the fortnightly one
Rai-	राई-	the morning one
Samvatsari-	संवत्सरी-	the major, annual one. Also, the last day of the *Paryushana*
Puja	पूजा	worship
Murti-	मूर्ति-	idol -
Punjabi	पंजाबी	a language or people of Punjab - a State in Northern India
Punya	पुण्य	effect of good deeds, opposite of *Papa*

Pura	पुर	a city
Vallabhi-	वल्लभी-	- of king Vallabha

Raga	राग	a liking, one of the 18 abodes of sin
Raja	राजा	a king
Rajashthan	राजस्थान	a State in Western India, just North of Gujarat.
Ramayana	रामायण	an epic dealing with the story of Lord Rama
Ratnatrayi	रत्नत्रयी	'Three Gems', viz. the true knowledge, the true understanding or perception, and the true character or behavior
Rupa Kosha	रूप कोषा	'treasure of beauty', the cortezan beloved of *Sthuli Bhadra*
Rushabha Deva	ऋषभ देव	the first *Tirthankara, Adishvara*

Sadhu	साधु	a monk (Sadh = to strive for)
Sadhvi	साध्वी	a nun
Samayika	सामायिक (correct)	a ritual lasting for 48 minutes, or two *Ghadis*
Samayika	सामयिक (incorrect)	a periodical magazine
Samsara	संसार	the worldly affairs, the cycle of births and deaths
-Davanal-dah	-दावानलदाह	the Sutra without any *Jodakshara*
Samudra	समुद्र	a sea, an ocean
Kshira-	क्षीर-	milk -
Samyag	सम्यग्	true
-Gnyana	-ज्ञान	- knowledge. One of the *Three Gems*
-Darshana	-दर्शन	- understanding or perception. One of the *Three Gems*
-Charitra	-चारित्र	- character or behavior. One of the *Three Gems*
Sangha	संघ	four part *Tirtha*, consisting of *Sadhus, Sadhvis, Shravaks* and *Shravikas*
Sanghavi	संघवी	(Guj.) a last name. One who has taken the *Sangha* on a pilgrimage generally to the holy city *Palitana*
Sanskrit	संस्क्रित	the English pronunciation of 'Sanskrut'

165

Sanskrut	संस्कृत	a language derived from Indo-European language. It is the mother of *Ardha-Magadhi, Pali,* and several modern north Indian languages. Sanskrut = civilized.
Sarasvati	सरस्वती	the goddess of learning, daughter of *Brahma*
Sazzaya	सज्झाय	self study, songs meant for self study, *Svadhyaya*
Shah	शाह	(Guj.) a king, here 'a king of a business', a common Jain last name
Bhama -	भामा-	- the loyal Jain minister of king Pratap, who gave up all his wealth to his king
Jagadu -	जगडू-	- the Shravak who gave up all his stored grains and wealth in the service of draught-stricken country
Moti -	मोती-	- the rich businessman who built many temples in Bombay, *Palitana*, etc.
Shila	शीला	a stone
Siddha-	सिद्ध-	a stone marker of *Siddhas* above a *Swastika*
Shakti	शक्ति	strength
Yatha-	यथा-	as. As your strength will permit, 'within your capacity'
Shankara	शंकर	Lord Shiva, the Hindu god of destruction. The great Hindu Acharya, who practically wiped out Jainism and Buddhism from India, about a thousand years ago.
-Acharya	-आचार्य	same as above
Adi-	आदि-	same as above. (Adi = first) many other Shankaracharyas succeeded him
Shanti	शांति	peace
-Natha	-नाथ	the 16th *Tirthankara*
Shatru	शत्रु	an enemy
Shatrunjaya	शत्रुंजय	one who has conquered his enemies, (Shatru = an enemy, Ji or Jaya = to conquer)
Mt.-	माउन्ट -	the holy mountain in *Palitana*
Shrarman	श्रमण	a tradition of Indian philosophy advocating renunciation, to which Jainism belongs; as opposed to the *Brahman* tradition

		which advocated sacrifice of animals to please the gods.
-Belagoda	-बेलगोडा	a town where a 60 feet tall statue of *Gomateshvaraji* or *Bahubaliji* is situated (literally, "monks' lake")
Sheth	शेठ	(Guj.) a businessman
Shethani	शेठाणी	wife of a businessman
Shiva	शिव	Lord Shankara, the Hindu god of destruction
Shravak	श्रावक	a Jain civilian man
Shravika	श्राविका	a Jain civilian woman
Shreemad	श्रीमद्	reverend
-Rajchandra	-राजचंद्र	a poet and saintly Shravak, who answered Gandhiji's questions, and guided him.
Shri	श्री	Mister, Mr., Babu.
Shudra	शुद्र	the lowest of the four castes, which includes the untouchables. Jainism does not believe in the caste system.
Shvetambara	श्वेताम्बर	Predominant sect of Jainism in which the monks wear white clothes, as opposed to *Digambaras* who wear no clothes at all
Siddha	सिद्ध	a liberated *Atma*
-Shila	-शीला	a symbolic representation of the *Siddhas* just above the *Swastika*
Stava	स्तव	a song of praise of the Jinas. Stu = to praise
Stavana	स्तवन	a song of praise of the Jinas. Stu = to praise
Sthana	स्थान	a place
Sthanaka	स्थानक	a place, an abode
Papa-	पाप-	abode(s) of sin, there are 18
Stotra	स्तोत्र	a song of praise of the Jinas. Stu = to praise
Stuti	स्तुति	a song of praise of the Jinas. Stu = to praise
Supana	सूपन	(Guj) a dream, *Swapna*
Suri	सूरी	a title for an *Acharya*
Sutra	सूत्र	a religious writing in verses. Sutra = a thread.
Kalpa-	कल्प-	the famous and holy *Sutra* dealing with the life Lord *Mahavira*, read during the *Paryushana*

Svadhyaya	स्वाध्याय	self study. Sva = self, adhyaya = study.
Swami	स्वामी	a master, *Natha, Prabhu, Ishvara*
Swapna	स्वप्न	a dream
Swastika	स्वस्तिक	a benevolent symbol, depicting the four directions that an *Atma* can take after the body dies, used as a reminder of our goal to break through that cycle of births and deaths. Swasti = May good come to you!
Tamil	तामील	a non - Sanskrit language, and also people of a region around Madras in southern India
Tapa	तप	a penance, to fast
Varasi-	वरसी-	an year long *Tapa*
Tapasvi	तपस्वी	a man who is doing a *Tapa*
Tapasvini	तपस्विनी	a woman who is doing a *Tapa*
Tirtha	तीर्थ	*Sangha*, consisting of *Sadhus, Sadhvis, Shravaks* and *Shravikas*
Tirthankara	तीर्थंकर	one who re-establishes a *Tirtha* or *Sangha*
Upadhyaya	उपाध्याय	a *Sadhu*, who teaches other *Sadhus*
Upashraya	उपाश्रय	a monastery where *Sadhus* and *Sadhvis* (in separate Upashrayas) live. (Upa- means Sub-, and Ashraya means a Shelter)
Upavasa	उपवास	a fast, during which the mind is turned towards the *Jinas*. (Up = Sub-, and Vas = to stay, that is, to stay in the viscinity of the Lord)
Vaishnava	वैष्णव	a follower of the Hindu Lord *Vishnu*
Vallabhipura	वल्लभीपुर	the city of king Vallabha
Varasi Tapa	वरसी तप	a year long *Tapa*
Vardhamana	वर्धमान	childhood name of Lord *Mahavir* ('Incremental', Vardha = to increase. With Lord's birth, the wealth, peace, etc. increased)
Varta	वार्ता	a story without any hidden message. Do not confuse this with *Vrata* (a vow).

Vartam<u>a</u>na	वर्तमान	prevailing, existing
-Joga	-जोग	set of circumstances, 'conditions permitting'
Vidhi	विधि	instructions or a recipe for rituals
Vih<u>a</u>ra	विहार	a Buddhist monastery
Chau-		(an unrelated word) a vow of not eating or drinking anything after sundown
Vimala	विमल	pure, clean, 'mud-less'
Vira	वीर	warrior, a brave one, a victorious one
Mah<u>a</u>-	महा-	great. The Great Victor
Virya	वीर्य	prowess, deligence, seminal fluid
Vishnu	विष्णु	the Hindu god who looks after the running of the world
Vrata	व्रत	an austerity, a vow. Do not confuse this with *Varta* (a story).
Yath<u>a</u>	यथा	as
-Shakti	-शक्ति	strenth. 'Within your capacity'

❈ ❈ ❈ ❈ ❈ ❈ ❈ ❈

INDEX

Please note that entries from the Treasure Chest are not included in the Index.

ORDERING INFORMATION

○ **ENGLISH FOR THE GRANDMA AND HER CHILDREN.** $ 15.00 each.
A stepwise course (in Gujarati) for those who do not know any English. Written in simple, easy to read style, in large types, for students of any age to learn English at their own pace. No rules, conjugations, or declensions to memorize. Includes a glossary and a list of commonly used phrases to facilitates communication during a stay in a hospital. Approx. 200 pages.

○ **A PROGRAMMED TEXT TO LEARN GUJARATI (2nd Edition).** $20.00 each.
The thoroughly revised one volume second edition of a very popular three part self-study classic (in English), adopted as standard text book by several teachers. Ideal for the new generation of Gujaratis, ten years and up, born and brought up in the U.S.A. and elsewhere, to help them learn to read and write in Gujarati. Approx. 300 pages.

○ **AN INTRODUCTION TO JAINISM (Second Edition)** $ 18.00 each.
Electronicaly produced 7 X 10" slightly smaller type version of the highly acclaimed first edition. Treasure Chest, Glossary, and Index are thoroughly revised, and typographical misprints are corrected. The content is otherwise preserved.

○ **AN INTRODUCTION TO JAINISM (First Edition).** $ 15.00 each.
A highly acclaimed, simple introduction to Jainism (in English), especially for the new generation of Jains, written in a clear and friendly style, full of explanations, and a gradual, stepwise presentation of the fundamental principles. For personal or classroom study. Equally interesting for non Jains of either Indian or Western origin, and for students and scholars of non-violence, vegetarianism, and ecology. Approx. 200 pages, 8.5 x 11". Only while the supply lasts. Call to check for availability.

○ **A CRASH COURSE TO LEARN THE GUJARATI SCRIPT.** $ 03.00 each.

○ **A CRASH COURSE TO LEARN THE DEVANAGARI SCRIPT**
(for HINDI, MARATHI, AND SANSKRIT LANGUAGES). $ 03.00 each.

A very concise introduction, only about 20 pages long, to Gujarati or Devanagari scripts (in English) for those who are too busy to learn by reading a big book, or by attending classes. One can learn to write one's own name, and that of one's family members, in a matter of couple of hours.

○ *SANSKRIT. AN APPRECIATION WITHOUT APPREHENSION.* $ 15.00 each.
For those who love Sanskrit, but are turned off by its complicated grammar. An introduction to the delightful language of scriptures and classical literature, and the mother of our mother tongues. Understand and appreciate all the classics, prayers and Subhashitani without any pain of remembering the complex rules. Includes the Crash Course to Learn Devanagari Script. Appr. 200 pages. *Due 2003.*

○ *PRICE AND DISCOUNT (overseas inquiries are welcome)*
    1-9   books   No discount
    11   books, and more   Pay for ten, get one free

○ *SALES TAX* New York State residents add 8.5 % to the amount.

○ *SHIPPING AND HANDLING* *(Within the U.S.A.)*
    $ 2.00   for single copy of any Crash Course.
    $ 3.00   for each book.
    $ 12.00   per every eleven book or a fraction thereof.

(PLEASE USE THE ORDER FORM ON THE OTHER SIDE)

ORDER FORM

Please review the information given on the other side carefully before preparing this order form. Check below the items that you wish to order. All orders must be accompanied by payment.

	TITLES	PRICE	NUMBER	AMOUNT
❏	English for the Grandma and Her Children	$15.00	....	$....................
❏	A Programmed Text to Learn Gujarati	$20.00	....	$....................
❏	An Introduction to Jainism (2nd Ed)	$18.00	....	$....................
❏	An Introduction to Jainism (First Ed)	$15.00	....	$....................
❏	A Crash Course To Learn The Gujarati Script	$03.00	....	$....................
❏	A Crash Course To Learn The Devanagari Script	$03.00	....	$....................
❏	Sanskrit. An Appreciation Without Apprehension (Inform when ready).			

Sub Total number of books. .... $....................

Sales Tax 8.5 % of the sub total
(New York State Residents only) $....................

Shipping and Handling $....................

GRAND TOTAL *(Payable to Setubandh Publications)* $....................

SHIP THE ORDER TO *(Please Print Clearly):*

Name:...

Address:..

City...................................State............Zip................-..............

Country......................Phone # (.........) ....-........................

Setubandh Publications
1 Lawson Lane
Great Neck, NY. 11023-1042. U.S.A.
(516) 482-6938.